W9-AZA-543

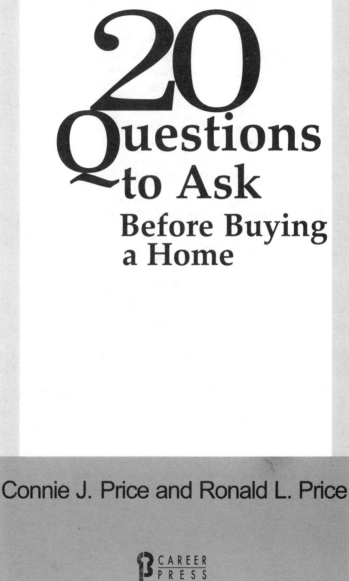

20 Questions to Ask Before Buying a Home

Connie J. Price and Ronald L. Price

CAREER PRESS

THE CAREER PRESS, INC.
Franklin Lakes, NJ

Copyright © 2005 by Ron and Connie Price

All rights reserved under the Pan-American and International Copyright Conventions. This book may not be reproduced, in whole or in part, in any form or by any means electronic or mechanical, including photocopying, recording, or by any information storage and retrieval system now known or hereafter invented, without written permission from the publisher, The Career Press.

20 QUESTIONS TO ASK BEFORE BUYING A HOME
EDITED BY KATE HENCHES
TYPESET BY KRISTEN PARKES
Cover design by Lu Rossman/Digi Dog Design
Printed in the U.S.A. by Book-mart Press

To order this title, please call toll-free 1-800-CAREER-1 (NJ and Canada: 201-848-0310) to order using VISA or MasterCard, or for further information on books from Career Press.

The Career Press, Inc., 3 Tice Road, PO Box 687,
Franklin Lakes, NJ 07417
www.careerpress.com

Library of Congress Cataloging-in-Publication Data
Price, Ron, 1947-
    20 questions to ask before buying a home / by Ron Price& Connie Price.
        p. cm.
    ISBN 1-56414-820-3 (paper)
        1. House buying—United States. 2. Residential real estate—Purchasing—United States. 3. Mortgage loans—United States. I. Title: Twenty questions to ask before buying a home. II. Title: Questions to ask before buying a home. III. Price, Connie, 1956- IV. Title. V. Series.

HD259.P75 2005
643'.12--dc22

                                                                2005042170

Contents

Introduction

Welcome Homebuyer!

A house is made of walls and beams;
a home is built with love and dreams.
—Anonymous

Owning a home has personal, cultural, and social benefits. According to a number of studies, owning a home has at least the following benefits:

- ➲ On average, homeowners appear to have better physical and mental health than renters.
- ➲ Homeowners are far more likely to vote than renters.
- ➲ Homeowners seem to have a lower divorce rate than renters.

- ⮒ Homeowners are more likely to be involved in their communities and attend church (although neither of which are actually required).
- ⮒ On average, homeowners' children are likely to have fewer behavioral problems in school.

There are also a few financial benefits to owning a home:

- ⮒ Owning a home can increase your savings.
- ⮒ Mortgage interest payments are tax deductible.
- ⮒ The profit from selling a home may be sheltered up to $250,000.

These benefits are on top of the basic benefits of owning a home: a sense of belonging, the freedom to exercise your creativity, and picking and managing your own environment.

Obviously, you are considering the purchase of a house—we mean *home*—or you wouldn't likely be reading this. However, it is also fairly obvious that you're not sure just how to go about it or what's involved in the process.

From the outside looking in, the home-buying process can be a bit frightening. On top of this, when you are buying a home, you are making what is likely the largest financial decision of your life. Needless to say, that alone can be terrifying. Believe us, we understand your plight and can reassure you that if you understand the process itself, your role in the process, and your rights throughout the process, buying a home may actually be tolerable, if not enjoyable, and after you've purchased your new home, it can be very satisfying indeed.

In this book, we have posed 20 questions that all new homebuyers should ask of themselves and of the professionals involved in the home-purchase process. We realize that our answers may not directly answer every question you might have, but we have tried to anticipate any other questions you might have and included detailed information and simple step-by-step instructions. To help ensure that you have the information you need, we have also listed other sources you can use to get more information, where appropriate.

To assist you through the home-buying process, we have included many checklists, real-life examples, and step-by-step to-do lists to help ensure that you don't overlook any vital step and that the purchase of your home goes as smoothly as possible.

As accurate and specific as we've tried to be, we realize that things do change and we welcome your comments and feedback. Should you wish to share information with us, please e-mail us at 20questions@comcast.net.

We truly wish you the best success in finding your home and only hope that we have made this process just a bit easier for you.

Happy house-hunting and we hope you enjoy your new home!

Connie J. Price
Ronald L. Price

Q*uestion* 1

Am I Ready to Buy a Home?

To some, the idea of buying a house, condominium, cooperative, or the like, is based on the conventional wisdom that *everyone* should own a home. But, as blasphemous as it may sound, should everyone own a home? To put it a slightly different way—is homeownership really right for everyone? And more specifically, is buying and owning a home really right for you?

We'll bet that you have had or will likely soon have a period in your life when it seems just about everyone is telling you that you really have to buy a home. "You're just throwing your money away paying rent," or one of its many variations is the typical advise everyone—from Dad, Mom, your older (and possibly younger) siblings, Uncle Bob, Aunt Sally, and even Grandma and Grandpa—has for you.

They must be right; and you really want to buy a home, don't you?

We agree that buying a home may not be exactly right for everyone. Whether or not right now may be the best time to buy a home depends on a variety of factors, some you control and some you don't. Let's take a look into the reasons you should buy a home and some of the arguments against buying a home at this time.

Why Buy a Home?

The reasons you are likely hearing for buying a home are:

➲ Paying rent is just like throwing your money away.

➲ Buying a house is one of the best and safest investments you can make.

➲ Home prices continue to increase and you should buy a house before the prices increase any more than they already have.

➲ Interest rates are lower than they have been in decades and you should buy before inflation causes rates to rise to the double-digit levels of the 1970s.

➲ Buying a house provides you with a tax deduction.

Let's look at these one at a time:

Rent versus Buy

Let's agree on one thing before we go any further: you need shelter in any case. So, either paying rent or paying on a mortgage provides the same benefit in that regard. In reality, you are not really throwing away your money when you make rent payments, you are merely paying for shelter.

As a renter, you receive two major benefits: you can easily change where you live and you are free of the responsibility for upkeep, repairs, and maintenance. A homeowner is the landlord and must ensure that any and all repairs and maintenance are performed. However, if you decide to move, it is definitely more complex to sell a home than to vacate a rented apartment or home.

Investing in a Home

Owning a home can provide a hedge against inflation and may even prove to be a great investment. However, what's true in one part of the country, or even in one part of town, may not be true in others.

As you make mortgage payments, each payment contributes to the equity of your home. Because your mortgage is leveraged, the value of your initial investment will, in most cases, continue to grow.

> *Just because home values inclreased in the past, there is no guarantee that values will continue to increase in the future.*

Leverage

When you purchase a home by investing only a portion of the purchase price (your down payment), your investment is leveraged. If you put down $40,000 (in earnest money and a cash down payment) on a $200,000 home loan and the value of the home increases only 10 percent, your investment has grown by 50 percent.

You should remember that just because home values have increased in the past, there is no guarantee that values will continue to increase in the future. Yes, although there's no guarantee that prices and values will continue to rise, it is very likely that demand will continue to outpace supply, which should keep upward pressure on home prices.

However, you should also consider that when interest rates are declining, home prices typically rise. Because you are able to buy more house (pay a higher purchase price at the same monthly payment), house prices tend to heat up just a bit. As a buyer, you are constantly trying to time your home purchase to the right combination of interest rates and home prices, which can be something like a teeter-totter.

The tax benefit of owning a home is often misunderstood.

Tax Breaks

The tax deduction you get on your federal tax return from a home mortgage is certainly better than the one you get from a rental payment. However, the tax benefit of owning a home is often misunderstood by many homebuyers.

In effect, you are allowed to deduct all of the interest and points paid on a home mortgage loan, any property taxes paid, and the net amount of any causalities or damages to your home. However, you must itemize your deductions to receive any benefit.

For the tax year 2004, the standard deduction for a married couple filing jointly was $9,700, which means they need to have more than $9,700 in itemized deductions (including home mortgage interest and property taxes) to gain any tax benefit at all.

Renters receive the $9,700 standard deduction regardless, which may or may not exceed the total of their rent payments. However, if a homeowner pays $20,000 in interest, fees, and taxes for his or her home, this amount (plus any other deductions claimed) could lower his or her taxable income considerably.

Because you typically have to pay to live somewhere anyway, any positive tax benefit should be looked at as an added bonus. All by itself, the income tax break really isn't compelling enough of a reason for you to buy a home.

Putting Off Buying a Home

Even if you have the financial ability to purchase a home, there a few reasons why you may not want to do so at this time. Some of the reasons why you might want to wait are: recent credit problems, such as a recent bankruptcy, a period with late payments, or simply too much debt; you have just graduated from college or there is a chance for a transfer or a promotion at work; your lifestyle isn't exactly right for homeownership; your marital status is unsure; you are new to an area; or you may not be able to remain in the home long enough for the home to appreciate.

Question 2

Is My Lifestyle Right for Homeownership?

There is a saying among Realtors that the three most important factors of real estate are location, location, and location. If this is true (and it is) then the next three most important factors are lifestyle, lifestyle, and lifestyle.

Renter's Lifestyle

People rent an apartment or house for a handful of reasons: cost, convenience, temporariness, and the ease to move in or out. For these reasons, a rented home best supports their lifestyle at this particular point in their life.

For many people, the "dream" of owning their own home has become more self-defined and customized around their personal wants, needs, and their financial and lifestyle objectives. For these people, renting, with its flexibility and freedom from obligation, can be a more appropriate housing option.

Is Homeownership Right for Me?

For some people, rental housing just makes sense—period. However, this is not the case for everyone. To determine whether you are really ready to buy a home or should rent, take the test at The Real Estate Center at Texas A&M University (*recenter.tamu.edu*). Answer the questions honestly; the test score can help you decide whether or not you're ready to take the plunge into homeownership.

Question 3

Are My Finances and Credit Adequate?

Buying a home, regardless of whether you already own one or are looking to buy your very first home, can be something like playing miniature golf. Each time you try to get started, there are obstacles in your way, such as credit status requirements, debt-to-income ratios, down payments, points, origination fees, and so on. Like the windmill hole on the mini-golf course, timing and skill (and luck) are needed to succeed. However, the key to success when buying a home is preparedness and being realistic about your needs and your ability to pay.

The Mortgage Market

When it comes to qualifying for a home mortgage, Gilster's Law says, "You never can tell; and it all depends." This is the standard answer to the question of whether you make enough income to qualify for a mortgage—the most essential step in buying a home for most people. What lenders feel is important isn't necessarily how much money you *make*, but rather how much money you have *left over* after you pay your bills.

What's important to lenders is that you have the ability to repay the loan, now and in the future. Banks, savings and loans, and credit unions are fairly conservative with their money and, as a result, they closely scrutinize your ability to pay the money back.

Most institutions require you to qualify under the guidelines of the Federal Home Loan Mortgage Corporation (commonly known as Freddie Mac) or the Federal National Mortgage Association (Fannie Mae). Other lenders, called portfolio lenders, typically have more flexibility and can qualify a borderline application when other lenders won't or can't.

> *Your ability to pay is based on your finances, and your willingness is based on your credit history and debt repayment history.*

Qualifying for a Loan

Lenders have only one objective in mind when making a mortgage loan: to make a "good loan." A good loan in lender-speak is one made to a borrower who is both willing and able to repay the loan. If you are able to demonstrate that you have both the willingness and the ability to repay, then you are an attractive customer to many lenders, which puts you in a position of power when it comes to choosing a lender. Of course, the stronger your capability in either area serves to strengthen your borrowing position, just like the weaker your ability and willingness to repay appears, the weaker your bargaining power.

The underwriting process determines your ability and willingness to pay. Your ability is based on your finances, and your willingness is based on your credit history and past debt repayment history. However, qualifying for a loan and becoming approved for a loan are two distinctly separate situations. On the basis of your income and current debts, you may "qualify" for a loan, but becoming "approved" involves an analysis of your current financial status and your credit history.

While you may be well-qualified to purchase a $250,000 home, you may not be able to qualify for a home priced at $350,000. The loan amount you are able to qualify for depends as much on the price of the house as it does on the loan terms available on the mortgage market at the time you apply.

So, how do you figure the amount for which you can qualify? Each lender computes this amount slightly different, and many have mortgage loan calculators on their Website. You can find a good mortgage calculator on the BankRate.com Website at *www.bankrate.com/gookeyword/*.

Income Requirements

When lenders look into your financial status, they want to verify two money questions:

1. Is your income large enough to cover the payments and expenses related to the mortgage plus your existing and any future obligations?
2. Do you have enough cash on-hand to cover the down payment and closing cost expense requirements of the purchase?

Lenders calculate a Housing Expense (HE) ratio and an Expense ratio to determine if your meet their lending criteria. Here's how these two ratios are calculated.

Housing Expense Ratio

The Housing Expense ratio, or *front ratio*, creates a percentage between your projected total mortgage payment, which includes the mortgage principal and interest (P&I), mortgage insurance (PMI), property taxes and hazard insurance (reserves), and your gross monthly income. In other words, your projected mortgage payment is divided by your total monthly income before taxes.

Total Expense Ratio

The Total Expense (TE) ratio, or the Maximum Expense ratio, is calculated very much like the Housing Expense ratio, except that your total monthly bills (including the proposed mortgage payment) are divided by your gross (before tax) monthly income.

Typically, the standard maximum for a TE ratio is 36 percent. With a 41-percent TE ratio, the borrower would not qualify for the mortgage loan he or she is seeking. However, TE ratios do vary among lenders, so if your TE ratio is at or just above the 36-percent limit, assuming you meet the HE ratio standard, you may want to try another lender.

Closing the Ratio Gap

If your situation is similar to the borrowers in the preceding example, there are ways to "fix" (meaning lower) your ratios. Price's Law of Mortgage Application says that a borrower with higher ratios has two choices when applying for a loan: "Raise the bridge or lower the river." What this means is that you can either come up with more income or you can find a house with a lower price or lower your monthly debt payments.

Lenders do, on occasion, raise their ratio maximum, but only in certain cases. If you find yourself in one of the following situations, you may want to ask your lender to reconsider a disapproved loan application.

➲ If you are just a point or two above the HE ratio, but comfortably below the TE ratio.

➲ If you have an outstanding credit record, such as a FICO score above 750.

➲ If you are a first-time homebuyer and you have made rent payments without fail for the past three years that amount to 40 percent, or more, of your total gross income.

➲ If you are making a down payment larger than the minimum required by the lender.

Raising the Term

If a borrower is turned down for a loan because of his or her HE or TE ratios, one last solution may be to increase the term length (number of payments) of the loan. However, 35 or 40-year terms may not lower the payment enough to provide much relief. If the borrower applied for a 15-year mortgage, raising the term length to 30 years can cut the monthly mortgage amount sufficiently to change the expense ratios and allow the borrower to qualify. Here are a few payment examples for a $300,000 loan at 6 percent for different terms.

Term Length	Mortgage P&I Payment
15 years	$ 3,375
20 years	$ 2,866
25 years	$ 2,577
30 years	$ 2,398
35 years	$ 2,281
40 years	$ 2,201

How Lenders Grade Borrowers

Just like the grades your teachers gave you in high school, lenders grade borrowers based on their credit (FICO) score and their credit performance. And like your school grades, you can be awarded an "A," "A-," "B," "C," "D," or "E" with an A the best and an E the worst. With an "A" grade, you get the best rates and lower loan points. A "B" score will add up to 2 percent the interest rate and require higher points. Scores of "C" or lower raise the interest rate even further and require pre-payment penalties.

A history of on-time payment is perhaps the best way to keep your credit rating healthy. Your credit score is what is used to determine your ability to understand the terms of the loan and your willingness to follow those terms in repaying the loan.

Q*uestion* 4

How Do I Choose the Best Location?

Choosing the right location for a new house is mostly a matter of personal preference, taste, and social status issues. However, finding just the right combination of features in a neighborhood that is in-town, out-of-town, urban, rural, or suburban, close-in, near shopping, or near schools (among other factors) is the challenge of finding just the perfect house.

Location, Location, Location

It's true that the location of a house can dramatically increase or decrease its value, regardless of its size, features, and condition. A $500,000 house in Southern California placed on a comparable lot in Paducah, Kentucky, would very likely only be valued at around $200,000. Where a house is located is by far the most important part of its valuation. While the differences may not be as dramatic as this example, even different sections of a town or city can vary the value of a house significantly.

When considering the location of a property, what the appraisers call its *situs*, your best rule-of-thumb is to buy the most house you can afford in the best location possible. Another version of this is to buy the worst house on the best street. In either case, you should have the best chance of reselling it, should you need to, and because of its desirable location, its value should remain strong. Remember that if the house needs repairs, updating, or remodeling, these improvements can only bring the house to the market values of the neighborhood, but not beyond. Buying the best house in the best neighborhood means that you are buying at the top of that market, and any improvements or additions made to the house likely will not increase its market value much, if at all.

Looking for the Bargains

If you are buying a home to live in for a relatively longer time (say 10 years or more), there are bargains on the market that can provide you with both shelter and, in the long run, an investment.

The characteristics that can help you identify a bargain home are:

- ⊃ A modest home on an expensive street (actually, this is more of an excellent investment than it is a bargain).
- ⊃ An otherwise well-maintained home that is untidy or unkempt.
- ⊃ A house being sold because of a family distress situation (such as divorce, death, financial crisis, or serious illness).
- ⊃ A home that has been improved beyond its neighborhood.

Investments versus Shelter

Housing costs have two parts: shelter costs and investment costs. Buying a house provides shelter (just as renting does), but it also provides an opportunity to build equity.

Investment Risk

A house, like any other investment, involves risk. There is the risk of a natural disaster (floods, hurricanes, tornados, earthquakes, and so on), fire, vandalism, and social or economic decline in an area. Insurance can help to safeguard your investment against natural disasters, fire, or vandalism, but there aren't any safeguards for your investment should the neighborhood decline.

Insurance can help to safeguard your investment.

Is a Home an Investment?

There is an ongoing debate in the housing market as to whether a home, meaning a house in which you live, is an investment at all. Some people (including us) contend that real estate investments are made only in properties you rent or lease to other people; your home may appreciate in value, but generally only enough to keep pace with inflation.

For most people, buying a house can be worth the up-front expense and increased costs in the longrun. However, in the shortterm, a house may not appreciate in value sufficiently to provide enough of a return to cover the costs should you decide to sell it. If you were to purchase a $300,000 home and invest around $42,000 in up-front costs (down payment and closing costs), it needs to appreciate around 11 percent before you could begin to break even on the deal. How so? When you go to sell your home, you will have selling costs of around 10 percent of the sale price.

Depending on the appreciation rate for the location of the house, this could take anywhere from a few months to several years. In high demand areas, it is possible to sell a house in a relatively short time and realize a nice return on your investment. However, the national average is very consistent with the rate of inflation, which is somewhere between 1 and 3 percent per year.

When you buy a home, remember that you are primarily buying shelter. Secondarily, you are investing in an asset that may increase in value enough to pay back your initial investment and perhaps a bit more.

Equal Housing Opportunity and You

Beginning with the Civil Rights Act of 1866 through and beyond the Fair Housing Act of 1988, it is illegal in the United States to discriminate against someone because of race, color, national origin, religion, disability, sex, or familial status in the sale or rental of property. The Fair Housing Act, the Americans with Disabilities Act (ADA), the Equal Credit Opportunity Act, and a wide range of state and local laws and ordinances prohibit the exclusion of anyone from the sale or rental of housing based on any criteria other than financial and credit qualifications.

It is illegal in the United States to discriminate against someone because of race, color, national origin, religion, disability, sex, or familial status in the sale or rental of property.

31

Home Sellers

Home sellers, landlords, and their agents cannot discriminate in the sale, rental, and financing of housing because of race, color, religion, sex, handicap, family status, or national origin. A seller or landlord cannot instruct a real estate broker or agent to limit or impede the sale or rental of housing. Nor can a seller or landlord include discriminatory terms or conditions in the purchase or rental agreements associated with a property.

Real Estate Brokers and Agents

Real estate brokers and agents are also bound by the law not to discriminate against either buyers or sellers in the sale of a home. Brokers and agents that belong to the National Association of Realtors (NAR) also subscribe to a Fair Housing Program that provides guidance to its members to ensure that discrimination has no part of the real estate buying and selling processes.

Homebuyers

As a home seeker, you have the right to expect that sellers and their agents will act in accordance with all civil rights and housing laws. Under these laws, you have the right to fully expect:

- ➲ No discriminatory limitations, exclusions, inclusions, or pricing in a community or location for housing.
- ➲ Equal representation from professional service providers.
- ➲ Access to the full range of housing choices in an area.
- ➲ No discrimination in the appraisal, closing, financing, and insurance of housing.

➲ Reasonable accommodations for persons with disabilities under the ADA.

➲ The freedom to exercise your fair housing rights without harassment or intimidation.

Choosing a Location That's Right for You

Sometimes the most desired neighborhood may not be so desirable under close examination. On the other hand, a seemingly marginal neighborhood might suddenly be just the right place.

Jack Harris, Mark Baumann, and Charleen Knapp of the Real Estate Center at Texas A&M University (*recenter.tamu.edu/ hguide/HBLocaList.html*) have developed a location checklist to help you narrow your search for just the right location. Use it as a guide to help you identify the location that best suits your needs.

Question 5

What About Building a Home?

One of your housing choices is to build a new home instead of buying an existing home. However, this choice does add some complexity to the process, depending on how much control you wish to have over the construction phases.

The General Contractor

The overall supervisor for a home construction project is the general contractor. This person monitors the schedule, hires and manages the subcontractors, and is responsible for ensuring the structure that is built meets (or exceeds) the requirements of the homeowners. The homeowners can serve as the general contractor, which can save some money, or they can hire a general contractor or homebuilder.

Hiring a General Contractor

A licensed general contractor knows the national and local building codes and has experience with the control and coordination of all of the materials, subcontractors, and inspections required to build your home, as well as how to handle the minor emergencies that are typical to any construction project. To understand just what a general contractor does, here are a few of the tasks involved:

- ➲ Getting competitive bids from subcontractors.
- ➲ Scheduling subcontractors.
- ➲ Developing the work schedule.
- ➲ Enforcing schedule and sequence of tasks.
- ➲ Supervising subcontractors and ensuring their work meets the homebuyers' expected standards.
- ➲ Obtaining local construction, electrical, plumbing, and other permits.
- ➲ Excavating, leveling, and preparing the lot for the home's foundation or concrete slab.
- ➲ Installing the foundation or slab and the driveway and walks.
- ➲ Connecting the water and sewer systems of the house to the public systems, or installing a septic system and drilling a water well.
- ➲ Coordinating with the public utilities companies and connecting the electrical or natural gas systems.

In addition, an experienced general contractor has a "history," meaning that he or she has built other houses and has references that can be checked and verified. The contractor also knows the local subcontractors: and which ones are reliable and produce quality work and should have the necessary insurance and bond to cover any accidents or injuries that may occur on the job, protecting you by limiting your liability.

Contracting the Job

Before you sign a contract with a general contractor, you should check the references and work of the contractor to ensure his or her reliability, trustworthiness, and the quality of his or her work. Verify his or her licensing; contact references; check with governmental or private consumer protection organizations for complaints against the contractor; and get written estimates and bids. One source for information on what you should expect from your contractor is the local association of homebuilders.

Financing a Home-Building Project

There are several options to financing a home-construction project, but most construction loans are typically either construction-to-permanent loans or end-of-construction loans.

Before signing a contract, check the contractor's references.

Construction-to-Permanent Loans

If your construction agreement requires periodic payments to the general contractor while the house is being built, a draw-type construction loan is best. When you take a draw loan, the "closing" for the mortgage occurs up-front, prior to construction starting. During construction, you pay only interest payments on the amount that has been drawn. The interest rate paid during construction is typically the same as on the total mortgage after construction, if the loan includes a conversion option. Many draw-type loans become due when the "certificate of occupancy" is issued and must be paid off from the proceeds of a standard mortgage.

End-of-Construction Loans

If the general contractor does not require progress payments during construction, an "End" loan is probably best for you. This type of loan disburses its funds when construction is completed. There are no interest payments during construction and your payments don't start until you receive your "certificate of occupancy." When the certificate is received, the interest is locked in, but, during construction, the interest rate floats with the market.

Choosing a Building Lot

Although it is something of a cart-before-the-horse situation, many people pick out their dream-home house plan before they begin looking for a building lot; while others find a lot in the perfect location and then begin looking for a house that best fits the lot. Regardless of which approach you choose, there are some things to consider when choosing a building lot.

Perhaps the most important issues you should consider are (in addition to location and price, of course):

➲ Is the lot large enough for the type and size of home you wish to build? Will the size of the lot accommodate any development, city, county, or state mandated easements and setbacks and still have room for the home you wish?

➲ What easements, if any, are placed on the lot?

➲ Is the lot in a flood plain or does it have a risk of flooding?

37

➲ What are the compass directions of the lot?
Will the front of the house face south (into the
sun in North America)? What direction does
the prevailing wind blow?

➲ Are there any covenants, conditions, and
restrictions (CC&Rs) effective on the lot?
What is the zoning for the lot and those that
border it?

Q*uestion* **6**

Should I Use a Real Estate Agent?

When considering whether or not to use the services of a real estate agent to find your new home, you need to ask yourself if you have the time, information, experience, knowledge, and contacts to efficiently find your dream home by yourself. If you do and can, you also may want to consider how much better the task would be with some professional help.

Agent, Broker, and Realtor

Although the terms *real estate broker*, *real estate agent*, and *Realtor* are all used interchangeably for the most part, there is actually some difference among them.

➲ **Agent:** A real estate agent a is working professional licensed in the state in which he or she provides services. Real estate laws vary by state, which is one of the reasons there are only state licenses and no national real estate licenses. An agent must be licensed before he or she can represent customers and conduct real estate transactions. Real estate agents are typically affiliated with a real estate broker and serve as an agent of the broker in real estate transactions.

➲ **Broker:** A real estate broker is technically a professional who brokers the sale and purchase of real property for a fee. In a more commonly used definition, a broker is a real estate salesperson who has advanced professional experience and education and has, after some experience as an agent, taken and passed a licensing examination to become a broker.

➲ **Realtor:** A Realtor is a member of the National Association of Realtors (NAR). The NAR is a real estate trade association and its members agree to abide by its Code of Ethics, which is updated each year to remain current with the laws, customs, and practices. Brokers and agents are not required to belong to the NAR, or one of its state or local affiliates, but the vast majority of real estate professionals do.

Finding an Agent

Actually, it's fairly easy to find a real estate agent, if you aren't picky as to whom you get—just open the Yellow Pages to real estate and take your pick. Real estate agents try just about anything to build up clientele and name recognition in a market. However, like any product, the agents who advertise the most aren't necessarily the best for you.

When selecting a real estate agent there are some qualities and abilities the agent should have. Probably the most important is that the agent should be someone with whom you are comfortable and whose company you enjoy. The agent should also be someone who listens to your desires and doesn't limit the market to only the listed properties he or she has listed. The agent should also be someone you respect and trust, because you may have to share private financial and personal information. Your agent should listen to your needs and be able to help you identify the type of house for which you are looking, he/she should be available at times that are convenient to you; and he/she should be familiar with the parts of town or neighborhoods you desire.

> *Your agent should list your needs and be able to help you identify the type of house for which you are looking.*

Agent Services

The services that a licensed real estate agent can provide to a home seeker cover the full range of finding and buying a home. These services aren't limited to the following, but typically include those services discussed in the next few sections.

Locating a Home

After you know the amount you can (the amount for which you have been prequalified) and want (the amount you have in mind) to pay for a house, you and your agent can begin to locate those properties that fit your needs and desires the best. Your agent should have access to the local area multiple listing service (MLS), which details all of the properties for sale that have been listed with real estate brokers and agents.

Selecting a Home

You and your agent can look through the information from the MLS to prescreen the available properties before you strike out to view each house that has potential. Your agent has the ability to show you information about any house listed in the local MLS regardless of which agent or broker has the listing.

When you have narrowed down the selection of houses to one or two, this is when an experienced real estate agent can be very valuable. When you think you've found just the right house, it is common that you are excited, emotional, and ready-to-move; your real estate agent can remain objective and provide you with information that can be valuable to know before you finalize an offer on a house, such as utilities, zoning, schools, future construction, or other developments in the area that may affect the property (such as a new freeway or a road widening project), and so on. In addition, the agent can help you to focus on two very important aspects of buying a house:

➲ Is the house good for a home and a good investment?

➲ Is the house likely to have a good resale value should I later wish to sell it?

Negotiating a Purchase

Price isn't the only thing that can be negotiated when buying a house. There are a number of factors involved in the purchase and sale that can be worked out between the buyer and seller, including: financing terms, date of possession, whether improvements or repairs are included or excluded from the price, what furnishings or equipment are included or excluded in the price, and more.

Depending on the local real estate laws or regulations, the negotiation process begins when you and your agent prepare an "offer" to be presented to the seller and the seller's agent. Your real estate agent is your "agent" in this negotiation and works through the agent representing the seller to arrive at a purchase agreement to which both the seller and you, the buyer, can agree.

Your real estate agent can provide some guidance as to what is usual and customary in your area for the amount of earnest money you should pay in relationship to the amount of your offer.

Property Investigation

After your offer has been accepted by the seller, you have a certain period of time to assure yourself that you really wish to purchase the house. During this period, you should inspect the property very closely. Typically, the necessary inspections are performed by professional inspectors who are specifically trained and licensed in specialty areas. The inspections are meant to look for and identify any of a number of serious problems with a home that aren't typically apparent to the untrained eye. These inspections include: termites and other pests, foundation and water problems, roofing, septic tank and well, dry rot, and any asbestos or other dangerous fibers and gases, among others. Your real estate agent should be able to recommend local qualified professionals to do the inspections and provide written reports, as well as estimates on what it would take to remedy any problems found.

It is also recommended that you perform a "title search" to verify that the title to the property is unencumbered. This service is most commonly performed by a title company. Should there be any problems with the title, your agent can assist you in clearing any potential problems.

Inspections are meant to look for and identify any number of serious problems ...that aren't apparent to the naked eye.

Financing Options

Once you are sure that you wish the purchase of the property to proceed, you next need to start or continue the financing of the property. If you are preapproved by a certain lender, it may be easier to continue with that lender, but your agent can help you understand the terms being offered and which type of financing plan is best for you.

Closing

The culmination of the sale is the process called *closing* or *settlement* (in different parts of the country). Depending on your area, all or part of the closing is performed by an escrow company, a title company, a lawyer, or a closing agent. Rely on your real estate agent for guidance through the closing process. See Question 19 for further information about the closing process.

The Agent's Role

Some states require real estate agents to represent only one party in a sale, but others permit what is called dual agency. But, before we look at dual agency, let's take a closer look at the roles an agent can fill:

➲ **Buyer agent:** As a buyer agent (and some agents specialize in just this service), the agent represents only the interests of the buyer without any direct ties or responsibilities to the seller. Buyer agents focus only on working with the buyer to find the best property available.

➲ **Listing agent:** In the role of a listing agent, an agent lists a seller's house for sale and then represents the interests of the seller to all potential buyers and their agents.

➲ **Dual agent:** Not every state permits dual agency, in which an agent represents both the buyer and the seller simultaneously, because of the potential conflict of interest. Ask your agent about dual agency in your state and decide for yourself if this is something you wish to permit, that is, if the state allows it.

Commissions

Real estate agents and brokers are paid a percentage of the purchase price of the home for their services. Because it is only at closing that the funds are distributed, the buyer and seller agents are paid from the proceeds of the sale and the closing costs of the seller. The buyer typically has no responsibility for paying real estate agent fees.

Until you have worked with an agent to find your dream home or to sell a home, it may seem like the fees paid to an agent may be excessive to the amount of work involved. However, if you take a closer look at what an agent really does for you, the fees become far less excessive. In addition to researching the market by studying the MLS and visiting homes for sale, the real estate agent is available to you essentially 24/7 to answer your questions, show you property, and to assist you in anyway he or she can. In addition, agents are also paid for their experience, expertise, knowledge, contacts, and consulting services. As a buyer, these services are free to you and should you ever sell your home, you'll find the fees paid to the agents are more than earned, by and large.

The buyer and seller agents are paid from the proceeds of the sale and the closing costs of the seller

FSBO

There are homes in every market that are being offered "For Sale By Owner" (FSBO—pronounced "fizz-bow"). A

FSBO sale is one that is not being offered through an agent but by a private homeowner.

A seller who offers a home for sale by owner has confidence that his or her home has a number of characteristics that will enable it to sell quickly at the price he or she is asking. This seller believes that his home is in superior condition and in an excellent location, has excellent features, and has an asking price that is a fair value. And because the FSBO seller typically believes the home will sell fast, he or she sees no need to pay for the services of an agent or broker.

Those FSBO homes that are truly superior do move relatively quickly, but a significant percentage of FSBO sellers often list their homes with a real estate agent after a certain amount of time, depending on the market.

The downside of buying a FSBO home is that all of the services that would have been provided by your agent, you must now do yourself. If you have the knowledge and ability to carry out these tasks, then a FSBO sale may save you some money and, in many cases, afford you a bit more house. However, if you omit any of the steps of the evaluation and inspection process, you could end up with more problems than you anticipated.

If you wish to purchase a FSBO home, hire the services of a real estate attorney to guide you through the process. The cost of this service will be well-worth it in the long run.

Question 7

What Should I Look for in a House?

When you begin your search for a home, you should clearly know what you're looking for. Before you look at the first house in your search, you should take the time to write down your criteria and identify those characteristics or features that are absolutely must-haves and those that are nice-to-haves. Must-haves are the things you can't do without—the deal breakers. Nice-to-haves are those things that would be a nice extra, but you can live without them. In other words, must-haves are the features and characteristics you are willing to pay for and nice-to-haves are extras for which you are less likely to value and include in your price offer.

Curb Appeal

"Curb appeal" is a real estate term that refers to how a house and its lot appear to someone driving by or parked at the curb. As a general rule, a house that doesn't appeal to you from the curb is not likely to appeal to you on closer inspection.

What contributes to the good curb appeal of a house are things such as tidiness, fresh paint, appropriate colors, well-maintained landscaping, driveways and walkways in good condition, and a lack of permanent customization. Curb appeal is your first impression. If your first impression is unfavorable, it's very likely (and human nature) that you will have to be *very* impressed with the rest of the house to overcome your feelings. However, if a house has outstanding curb appeal, it is likely (again, human nature) that you will be more willing to overlook minor imperfections in the home.

When looking at properties, you shouldn't get too high or too low, meaning too impressed or too bummed out by what you see. Be objective and wear your poker face, but also listen to that little voice inside, it's usually right-on about what's right for you.

Floor Plan

You should identify your ideal floor plan before you actually begin looking. You should consider the needs of your family and each of its members and take a good look at how you live and in what part of the house will you spend most of your time. Ultimately, you may not find the exact floor plan you are seeking, but you may find a few that are very close. If you don't identify the floor plan you desire before you look, you will end up comparing apples to oranges, so to speak, instead of how closely each of a few houses comes to your ideal—a much easier choice to make.

Infrastructure

A house's infrastructure comprises the piping, paving, cabling, and services that are typically installed by third parties (other than you and the builder), such as the city, water or sewer district, cable TV company, and the like. The infrastructure is commonly owned or maintained under an easement held by the installer or regulator, otherwise it is considered a part of a home and must be maintained by its owner.

It is important to know what utility, sewer, water, and other basic services are connected to a house. While some of these services are apparent because of their meters (electricity and natural gas), tanks (propane gas and water softening), or pumps (water well), others may not be so obvious. Even if they seem evident, ask about the utility and service connections and sources to a house.

Features of a house such as driveways, sidewalks, and curbs are also a part of a house's infrastructure. Inspect these features and look for breaks, upheavals, lowered sections, and anything out of the ordinary. A broken sidewalk, especially on a newer home, indicates a problem with the materials, workmanship, or, among others, the ground underneath the concrete. If a section of a sidewalk or driveway is pushed up, creating a hazard, it is typically caused by the roots of a tree, which may not even be on the house's lot. If the driveway or walkways present a safety hazard, the homeowner is commonly responsible for its correction.

> *It is important to know what utility, sewer, water, and other basic services are connected to the house.*

You also want to be aware of services or utilities that are available (or not available) to the lot in case you wish to add a service or utility after taking possession. For example, if you plan to install a natural gas fireplace, you need to know if natural gas lines are available and whether they are available on or near the property. There is a fairly significant difference between a service or utility that is "to the lot" (meaning terminated at the edge of a lot) and one that is "in the street" (meaning that you must pay to have it brought onto a lot).

Exterior

There is more to a home's exterior than its color and the landscaping. A house can be like an iceberg; and, like an iceberg, you may only be able to see the tip or only the seemingly small and visible part of a problem. Anything that seems odd or out of the ordinary may be an indication of a problem and you should definitely be suspicious about it. *Never* assume anything away; ask about it—you are considering spending a few years' income on the house and you should never willingly put yourself in a position for surprises.

If you are seriously considering a house, look at it in every type of light and weather you can: sunny days, cloudy days, rainy days, and even at night. If the yard and roof are covered with snow, ask for pictures that show the yard uncovered in good detail; better yet, wait until the snow melts to inspect the yard and the house's exterior.

Anything that seems odd or out of the ordinary may be an indication of a problem.

Deferred Maintenance

Normal wear and tear can take its toll on a house, if routine maintenance is put off. If wear and tear is allowed to accumulate, small or minor issues can become large and costly to correct. Common examples of deferred maintenance are exterior and interior paint, broken fixtures, minor (yet visible) water damage, overgrown bushes and shrubs, weedy lawns, discolored or broken fencing, and the like. Don't confuse major faults or repairs with deferred maintenance. A deferred maintenance issue is typically relatively minor and easy to remedy.

There are situations where deferred maintenance can almost be expected, such as an elderly person living alone, a disabled person, or a house that has been vacant for a while. In these cases, especially, but in other cases as well, the deferred maintenance issues should be reflected in the price of the home.

Major Faults

Unless you are willing to take on problems with a home immediately, you should carefully inspect a home for major problems, such as foundation and roof issues, sunken areas in the yard (indicating potential septic or sewer issues), uneven flooring, older appliances, and so on.

You have to decide whether a house that otherwise meets your criteria is worth an additional investment of your time and money to correct a major problem. This is one of the reasons why you should hire a building inspector to look over a house on which you have made an offer, subject to inspection. This trained professional will be able to red flag any issue that may cause a snag in your financing or be a minor or major repair. You have to decide whether the seller should fix these items or if you are willing to take them on yourself.

After Purchase Modifications

If you find a house you like that meets all of your criteria, except for one or two fairly major items, you may decide that you like the house enough to purchase it and remodel it to add the features it's missing. Before you proceed with this plan, discuss it with your agent and the contractor you plan on using to do the work. There are building codes and regulations that may prevent you from remodeling the house in just the way you envision it. There may also be infrastructure issues that would cause the project to end up prohibitively expensive in the end.

Share your plans for any remodeling you may wish to do on a house after its purchase with your agent and, if applicable, your real estate lawyer. Remember that these people are experienced and knowledgeable professionals. They have very likely been through exactly what you are proposing once or twice and most likely have some very valuable (and free) advice and expertise that could allow you to avoid a costly mistake.

Q*uestion* 8

What Questions Should I Ask About a House?

?

If you are working with a buyer's agent, normally you would have no or very limited interaction with a seller. Any and all of your questions would be channeled through your agent, who would work with the seller's agent to get you the information you are seeking. Of course, if you are considering a For Sale By Owner (FSBO) house, your questions are addressed directly to the seller. In either case, the questions you should ask are much the same.

Why Is the House for Sale?

Your agent will most likely be ahead of you in asking this question. Knowing the buyer's motivation and his of her urgency to sell can be a great bargaining point. A seller who is looking to "move to the country" isn't likely as motivated to sell as a seller who is going through a divorce, relocating, has been laid off, or suffered another type of hardship. A motivated seller is more willing to make a deal than one who's not.

On occasion, what you and your agent are told may not be completely true, but when you are looking at a house, there may be a few clues as to the seller's real motivation: women's clothing, but no men's; stacks of packed boxes in the garage or basement; unfurnished or unusually sparsely furnished rooms; or perhaps a vacant house. Although these can all be explained away, you and your agent should be able to interpret them and use them to formulate your offer, should you wish to make one.

What Did the Seller Pay for the House?

The price the seller originally paid for the house is recorded as public information that is available to anyone who wishes to know. Your real estate agent typically has ready access to this information. This is good to know because it provides information about the amount of equity the home has built up and in what amount of time. A seller that has been in a house for some time and has built up some equity is more likely to consider a lower offer than someone who has been in a house for only a short time.

> *The price the seller originally paid for the house is recorded as public information.*

What About the Neighborhood?

The neighborhood, as much as the house, should support your lifestyle as well. If you have young children, are there other families with young children? If you have pets, are there other families with pets in the neighborhood? Are all of the cars parked next door always there?

What are the issues in the neighborhood that may prove to be a problem for you? By asking more specific questions, you are more likely to get better answers. Sellers, in general, may be forthcoming with information about a house, but they may be less likely to share what they deem to be negative information about the neighborhood. So, ask your questions and keep asking them until you are satisfied with the answers.

It's also a good idea to visit the neighborhood by driving by or walking through it at different times of the day. You may even want to chat with your potential neighbors about what they like or don't like about the neighborhood and if they know of any particular problems with the house you are considering.

What About the Schools?

If you have school-age children or are yourself interested in attending a college or university, you may wish to know the relative location of the house to the local schools or colleges.

For many buyers, the quality of the schools is often a priority. These buyers may choose the school district and then begin looking for an appropriate house within that area. How you judge the schools, if this is a priority, is up to you, but the sellers and real estate agents are likely to have opinions. However, if the seller's children attend private school, you may want to investigate why.

What Is the History of the House?

There are some things about a house's past that you should want to know. Has the house ever been a rental? Has there ever been major damage (flood, fire, weather) to the house? Has there ever been a major crime committed in the house? Some buyers will refuse to consider a house in which a death has occurred because they fear the house may be haunted. Talking with the neighbors may be the best way to learn about this part of a house's history.

Maintenance Questions

You should also ask questions about the condition of the house and its maintenance. How old is the roof? How old is the furnace and when was the last time it was cleaned? When was the last time the furnace was cleaned or checked for carbon dioxide (CO_2) leaks? Has the electrical system, especially the electrical circuit box, been updated, and, if so, when? Have any changes been made to the plumbing or heating systems; if so, when? Has the basement leaked in the past? Is there a sump pump installed? Has the house been tested for Radon? You should be absolutely sure you have all of the information you need about the home's central systems before making any judgments about the property.

It's Your Decision

When you are looking over a house with an interest to buy, it as a home for you and your family, so you cannot possibly ask too many questions. Don't rationalize your questions thinking that just because it's a brand new house doesn't mean everything is okay. Not everything is necessarily as it appears and you should really drill down into the infrastructure (heating, electrical, plumbing, lighting, paved areas, and so on) until you are completely satisfied that there are no problems or any problem that does exist is relatively minor (in *your* opinion; not the opinion of the seller, the seller's agent, or even your agent).

Question 9

How Can I Be Sure I've Found the Right House?

If you believe you have found the perfect, or at least a near perfect house, you should make an offer to buy it, right? Not so fast. There are still at least a couple of questions we'd like you to ask yourself before you make that final leap. Is the house right for you in the immediate future as well as in the long-term?

Immediate Needs

At the risk of repeating ourselves, the house you buy should fit your lifestyle, not only in the present but in the future as well. If you are a young couple with no children, the amount of house you need depends on how soon you plan on adding to your family. Why pay for more house than you will need in the near and intermediate terms? However, if you plan to have children or add other family members to the household in the not-too-distant future, then you should look for a house that will accommodate the additional people.

If you don't currently have pets, but would like to have a dog, cat, horse, pig, or even a herd of cattle at some point in the future, you should look at houses that can easily accommodate this desire.

Too Much House

Buying more house than you really need can mean more upkeep and expense than you may be planning on. Some areas that homebuyers fail to think about when they see a house that really appeals to them are:

- ➲ **Cleaning:** Unless you plan to close off part of the house and cover its furniture with dust cloths, like in the scary movies, you'll need to clean even unused parts of the house at least periodically.

- ➲ **Heating and cooling:** Perhaps the biggest single impact of having more space than you need is the financial burden of having to heat or cool the extra space, adding to your total cost of housing.

- ➲ **Insurance:** The cost of insurance is essentially based on the square footage of the house, along with its construction materials, features, accoutrements, and the cost to rebuild the house should it be destroyed. A larger house definitely costs more to insure than a smaller house.

- ➲ **Maintenance:** All houses need some regular maintenance and upkeep. Exterior areas need scraping, paint, caulking, and the like, unless the house is covered with vinyl siding. Interior spaces may need floor care, paint, window treatments, and more, especially if fashions and tastes change. Once again, the larger the space, the more maintenance and upkeep are bound to cost.

Not Enough House

Buying a house that is too small for your future needs can be as much of a problem as one that is too big. Perhaps not so much in monthly expenses, but too small of a house can certainly have an impact on your lifestyle and your total housing costs.

If you purchase a house that is just right for your immediate needs, but becomes too small as your family and lifestyle changes, it can prove to be a problem in the long run. Once the house becomes too small, you are faced with either selling the house and buying a bigger one, or adding onto your existing house. If you purchase a house primarily because of its location, you may not want to move to a new location. If you picked your house because of its floor plan or features, you could have a difficult time finding another just like it—only larger.

Adding onto and remodeling an existing house isn't always the easiest thing to do, given that you have to worry about easements, property lines, set-backs, zoning laws, and the like—not to mention the infrastructure of the house and whether it can support the added space.

It is far better to take a hard look at your life as it is today and how it is likely to be in the near, intermediate, and long-term future as best as you can. Buy the house that best fits your near-term and intermediate-term needs, and your long-term needs, if possible.

Adding onto and remodeling an existing house isn't always the easiest thing to do.

Long-Term Fit

You also need to consider, based on your plans for the next three to five, or more, years whether the house will continue to meet your needs should your family change, your lifestyle change, or even your life outside your family changes (and you really don't have control over it).

Some buyers think that they can grow into a house, which usually means, it doesn't fit their needs in the near term, but it could later. Other buyers think that a house that is just right now and (because the kids are going away to college next year) if the house becomes too big later, they can just sell it and move down, assuming the market stays healthy.

You should pick the house that is best for you right now and in the near future. Nobody knows what the future holds for sure. Unless you have a very good idea of the future, and you very well could, pick a house based on what you know, not necessarily on what you want to happen.

Q*uestion* 10

Is the House Really Right for Me?

Every house needs some improvements or repairs, even a brand-new house to a certain extent. From your inspections, you probably noticed some areas of possible neglect or deferred maintenance, some minor and perhaps some fairly major. Despite these shortcomings, as is often the case, there is enough about the house to like that these minor flaws or problems as set aside in the consideration of the home and whether it's right for you.

Obsolescence

In general, the three primary reasons why a house could drop in value over time are abuse, location, and obsolescence. Abuse is obvious in that a home may have holes in the walls, heavily scratched floors, extremely dirty carpets, and the like. Location, while often a major contributor to a home's increasing value, can also become a negative factor as well. The very best house in a declining neighborhood may or may not increase in value and may, in fact, decrease in value.

Obsolescence is often less obvious, especially to first-time home buyers who lack experience in what exactly to look for. There are two types of obsolescence that can affect the value or the desirability of a house: external obsolescence and functional obsolescence.

External Obsolescence

The factors that contribute to external obsolescence are typically beyond the control of the homeowner. External obsolescence is caused by the sensory perceptions of anyone viewing a house, whether a prospective buyer or an appraiser. Some of the factors that contribute to external obsolescence are:

➲ **Sameness:** In some housing developments, only a few house designs are used, which means that any one house probably resembles several other houses and perhaps one that is only a few doors away. Even the colors of the houses may be very similar. To a buyer looking for something unique or different (or something with at least its own identity), all of the houses looking the same can have a negative impact.

➲ **Pollution:** While there are very few locations like Love Canal and Three Mile Island, there are areas where the land either nearby or on which a house is built may be polluted from its previous use. In this context, pollution doesn't have to mean toxic waste, chemicals, or the like; it can mean dairy farm, landfill, or overhead high-tension electrical power lines. These factors, if they become an issue, can decrease the value of a property.

➲ **Neighbors:** Another example of external obsolescence is the neighbors on either one or both sides of a house keeping multiple cars, trucks, RVs, or trailers in various stages of disrepair in their yards. Or if the neighbors paint their home bright pink, or build a fence out of old car wheels, or decide to sell "pharmaceuticals" out of their garage. There isn't anything wrong with these actions necessarily, except maybe selling certain items, but they are so out of the ordinary that to sell a nearby house, the price may have to be lowered.

➲ **Vicinity:** Not all homebuilders are the best business people. This is often evident when a very nice development is placed so that you must travel through auto wrecking yards or the public landfill to get to it. Also, the recent addition of an interstate highway about a block away or a high-speed train is now using what you thought were abandoned rail lines. Also remember that the best house in the worst neighborhood is not likely to increase in value unless the neighborhood itself improves dramatically first.

Functional Obsolescence

When the design of a house fails to meet the requirements of the average homebuyer or has a generally poor design, style, or infrastructure, the house is said to have functional obsolescence. Functional obsolescence is a condition that can also impact the value of a house.

Functional obsolescence is caused by either one or more deficiencies or what is called super-adequacies. A house in Arizona that lacks air conditioning is functionally obsolescent for its deficiency. A house to which a large bird sanctuary has been added is super-adequate, typically beyond the needs of the average buyer.

Some examples of functional obsolescence are:

➲ A house with six bedrooms and one bathroom.

➲ In some parts of the country, a home with electric baseboard heating.

➲ Electrical power incapable of running several appliances at the same time.

➲ A house with an indoor swimming pool (quite often).

➲ A house within a city's limits not connected to city water and sewer.

➲ A house customized to resemble the Starship Enterprise.

We think you get the idea. Functional obsolescence can be caused by not only what a house doesn't have, but often by what it does have, as well.

Repairs

When you look at a house, you should carry paper and pen to note every single flaw you see. Try not to pass judgment while you are looking; just observe and record what you see. Sure, it is obvious at first sight that some houses aren't for you. However, on the houses you are really considering, take notes. In fact, you should sketch the floor plan and annotate your notes on it to help you remember what you saw.

In most cases, your notes will indicate any repairs or re-modeling projects that you wish the owner (seller) to perform as a condition of the sale or that you will take on should you purchase the house. Some common examples are: the deck needs to be cleaned and a broken rail repaired by the seller; the guest bathroom needs updating (something you would do after the purchase); the carpet in the dining room should be replaced (negotiable); or the seller should replace or repair a faulty light switch in the basement.

In a house that they otherwise like, many buyers have a tendency to rationalize most needed repairs as minor. However, a house with four or five "minor" repairs in each room could become a "major" project. Do you have the time, skills, or money to take on all of the needed repairs? Take a hard look at the big picture and be honest with yourself. Unless there are compelling reasons to the contrary, the amount of repair required may not be worth it.

Remodeling

Some buyers, especially those looking to buy in a particular location, often believe they can correct a house's shortcomings by remodeling it. Objectively, this is the same as saying that you are willing to pay more than the owner is asking for the house. Unless the owner is willing to discount the price to allow for the remodeling *you* wish to do, the cost of any remodeling is, in effect, part of the price you are willing to pay for the house.

Q*uestion* 11

How Much Should I Offer?

While your real estate agent can provide some guidance for you in what you should offer for a particular house, the amount you offer is ultimately up to you. You have to decide how much you really want the house. Your agent can help you to understand the number of other buyers that may be interested, but often there is no real way to really know for sure.

The amount you wish to offer for the house can of course be the full price or an amount higher or lower than the asking price. The objective of making your offer is to come up with the amount you feel to be a fair price for the house and the amount that represents what the house is worth to you.

There are services and information you can use to help you determine a price to offer for a house:

➲ Comparative market analysis (CMA).

➲ Property tax assessment.

➲ Professional appraisal.

Comparative Market Analysis

A CMA can be used to determine a fair market asking (listing) price for the seller or a fair offer amount for a buyer. Although you will see CMA defined as a "certified" market analysis by some agents, there is really nothing certified about it. A CMA is an informal analysis of the characteristics, features, and pricing of similar homes that have been sold, are pending a sale closing, or are currently on the market.

If you only wish to have a CMA done that compares the price of a certain property to those sold within the past year, you can get the same information as your agent from the county records in the tax assessor's office. However, understand that there can be a delay in the posting of this information, which may omit the very latest information from your analysis. Your agent has access to more current information in the multiple listing service (MLS), which would also include any sales that are currently pending. Pending sales can often reflect the current market conditions more than a sale completed more than six months ago, especially in a high-demand market.

Assessments

Property taxes are based on an estimate of a property fair market value as determined by the rules used by a city, county, or state tax assessor's office staff. Depending on where the property is located, one of three possible ways are likely used to estimate the fair market value of a property for tax purposes:

➲ **Cost:** Also called the reproduction method, the cost method estimates the value of the land first and then estimates the cost of reproducing any existing structures on the property. Typically, this method is used for business or special use properties.

➲ **Income capitalization:** This method is most commonly used to estimate the value of income producing properties, such as apartment buildings or office buildings. It is not used for single-family residential property.

➲ **Sales comparison:** This is the method most commonly used to estimate the tax valuation of single- to three-family houses. Essentially, the sale comparison method involves about what is used in a CMA: the sale prices of recently sold properties in the immediate area of a home. The cost or reproduction method is occasionally used when no houses have sold in an area for some time.

Assessment Value

Most states require properties to be assigned to one of three or four particular property classes. In this scheme, residential properties for one to three families are assigned to Class 1 or Class A status. The assignment to a tax class is important because each tax class carries a different valuation percentage, which is used to determine the tax base for a property.

Tax assessment percentages can vary anywhere from as low as 5 percent to 100 percent, which means, respectively, that only a small percentage of a property's value is considered for taxation or all of its current value is considered.

For example, in Cheshire County, New Hampshire, the fully equalized tax rate is $28.46 per one thousand dollars of the first 65.9 percent of the assessed market valuation of a residential property. The actual tax rate is $29.12, but it is equalized by a factor of 98.6 percent. So, the property tax for houses assessed at $200,000 in Cheshire County is calculated as follows:

($29.12 x 0.986) x [($200,000 / 1,000) x 0.659] = $3,751.00

Other jurisdictions use only a percentage of a house's value (for instance, 15 percent) but apply a higher tax rate, while others use the full (100 percent) value and apply a lower tax rate.

Appraisal

Don't confuse a CMA with an appraisal or an inspection. For one thing, a professional appraiser is certified and licensed in most states and is experienced in valuing a house based on its size, condition, quality, and functionality. An appraiser generates a detailed report that lists the good and bad characteristics of a house that were included in his or her valuation of the house. Like the real estate agent and the CMA, the appraiser also looks at how the house compares to similar houses in the area in determining a valuation. An inspection is used to identify any deficiencies in the home that may impact its value or functionality.

Lenders require an appraisal to establish the loan value of a house and to protect them from lending too much, but an appraisal can also protect the buyer from paying too much, as well. But, there is nothing preventing you from paying to have an independent appraisal done on a house to help you to determine its worth before making an offer. Of course, you will need the seller's permission to do so, but your agent should be able to arrange this. The cost of an appraisal (commonly between $300 and $500) can be like buying an insurance policy against making a bad deal.

The Cost of Repairs or Remodeling

If you have determined that a house is right for you, but it requires some extensive repairs and remodeling, there is a tendency among buyers to want to deduct the cost of the repairs and remodeling from their offer. While the cost of repairs (those the seller agrees to) can and should be deducted from a full-price offer, unless the offer is made contingent on the repairs being performed, the cost of remodeling probably should not be deducted. Remodeling a house is a personal preference in which the seller has no real interest. Any remodeling you want to do is strictly your wishes and not those of the seller.

Q*uestion* 12

How Do I Make an Offer?

Making an offer to purchase a home amounts to opening negotiations with the seller. You hope the seller accepts your price, but the seller actually can exercise two options: he or she can turn you down completely; or he or she can counteroffer with an offer proposal of his or her own. But, to ensure that your offer is valid, legal, and the seller is able to accept it, there are a few rules you must follow, regardless of which state you're in.

Making an Offer on a FSBO

To make an offer to a FSBO seller, you need to prepare and present three documents: a copy of a letter from a lender that states that you are preapproved for at least the offer you are making on the house; a signed purchase and sale contract (preferably from a real estate attorney), and an earnest money check. If the FSBO seller agrees to use a closing attorney or a title company to process the sale of the home, the earnest money check should be made payable and given to the attorney or closing agent. You should also demand the disclosure statements required by virtually every state that detail the condition of the house and any other information the seller knows about the property.

A FSBO seller is typically trying to avoid the cost of using a real estate agent, which means he or she may be trying to cut other cost or time corners as well. Stick to your due diligence plan and schedule the inspections you want and verify that this is actually the home you think it is. The real estate law in virtually every state allows you a reasonable amount of time to make inspections, title searches, and the other verifications you need in order to complete the sale. To be absolutely sure, make sure any and all inspections, searches, and verifications you wish to make are stipulated in the contract as contingencies to void the contract.

Making an Offer on a Listed House

When you wish to make an offer on a house listed by a real estate broker or agent, a definite formality and sequence of events that are prescribed by law must be observed and followed. The benefit of working with a real estate agent is that when you wish to make an offer on a house, the agent knows exactly what you need to do, which forms to use, and when to do what.

Forms

Every state has its own set of standard forms that must be used in a real estate transaction. Your real estate agent typically provides and fills out these forms for you. In fact, he or she should fill in the forms in your presence. Regardless of when the form is filled in, be sure you read every addition made to the form. These additions are generally hand-written entries made to blanks embedded in the form's language. The fill-ins are used to specify the exact amounts, numbers, conditions, contingencies, and requests that make up your offer.

The Offer

The basic information that should be included in an offer to purchase real estate is:

➲ **Proposed selling price:** The amount you're offering to pay for the house.

➲ **Concessions:** Any concessions you wish the seller to give (such as leaving appliances or furniture, performing cleanup, and so on).

➲ **Financial contingencies:** If the sale of the house is subject to you being able to obtain financing (a mortgage loan), you can stipulate the interest rate, terms, and amount, if you'd like. Remember that, in most cases, the buyer has only been preapproved.

➲ **Inspection contingencies:** This contingency typically specifies the amount of time the buyer has to arrange for an inspection to be performed and the amount of time the seller then has to correct any faults cited in the inspection report. You may also state that any faults will void the offer or you can say that any repair over a certain dollar amount voids the contract. Actually, you can deal with this (and all contingencies on the offer) just about any way you want to.

➲ **Sale inclusions:** The offer document must specify exactly what you believe you are making an offer to purchase. The term *real estate* generally refers to all items physically attached to the house and other structures on the property. But you shouldn't just assume that the seller understands this. You need to detail the items your offer includes, such as planter boxes, fireplace screens or doors, appliances, window-mounted air conditioners, window dressings and draperies, and the like. *When in doubt; spell it out.*

➲ **Earnest money:** The amount of earnest money deposited with the offer.

After your agent presents your offer to the seller, typically in the presence of the seller's agent, the seller has the amount of time you've specified in the offer to respond by accepting the offer, rejecting the offer, or making a counteroffer. The seller can also just let the offer expire.

The Offer Becomes a Contract

Once the seller has seen your offer, it is a pending offer and, at this point, nothing can be changed in the offer unless the seller rejects it, prepares a counteroffer, or allows the offer to expire past its review limit time period. Should the seller not accept your offer, your original offer can be modified some or completely, and be re-presented to the seller by your agent. Or you can just walk away and look for another property.

If or when the seller accepts your offer, you and the seller have reached an agreement on the purchase and sale contract. At this point, you have a few responsibilities, as was likely spelled out in the agreements.

Apply for Mortgage

Now that you know the house you wish to buy, you can take a copy of the purchase and sale contract to your mortgage lender and move your preapproval into a fully qualified approval for a mortgage loan in the amount you need to purchase the house.

The lender will determine your credit-worthiness, the amount you require to purchase the house, and if they are willing to loan you this amount of money. If you meet their current credit-worthiness and repayment requirements, your loan will likely be approved. Once you have been approved for a loan, meaning you can proceed, you should order the inspections you included in the contract.

Question 13

What if I Change My Mind?

When you make an offer on a house, secured with earnest money, and the offer is accepted by the seller, a binding contract is created under the real estate laws of virtually every state in the United States, and most of the rest of the world, as well. At minimum, if you decide to breach (break) this contract, you will likely forfeit the earnest money to the seller, but there could be more to it than that.

As the buyer, you have certain obligations in the contract, as does the seller. Breaching a contract can lead to litigation, which can be very costly. So, if you feel you really need to back out of a deal, think about its repercussions as well.

However, there are legal reasons that can allow you to back out of a purchase agreement. If the contract was contingent on inspection, financing, or perhaps even the sale of the buyer's existing home, both the buyer and seller may have valid reasons to void the deal.

Contingencies

If the offer to buy a house is made contingent on financing, the sale of an existing property, or inspection, the buyer (and, in some cases, the seller) may have the right to cancel the offer (void the contract) should any of these contingencies fail to complete to the buyer's satisfaction.

Financing Contingency

An offer made contingent on financing is typically made when the buyer hasn't been preapproved for a loan before making the offer nor has credit conditions that may make obtaining financing questionable. If this contingency exists and the buyer is unable to obtain financial (meaning approval for a loan) by a certain date or in a certain number of days, the contract can be voided.

Sale of Property Contingency

If the buyer has an existing house that is currently on the market or will be very shortly, it is common that the buyer cannot obtain financing for a new house without first selling the existing house. In this case, the buyer will want to make a contingent offer that is contingent on the sale of his or her existing house. The idea behind this contingency is that the buyer needs time to sell the existing house before closing.

Typically, a sale of property contingency is tied to a set number of days, such as 60 or 90 days, at which time, if the existing house is not sold, the buyer defaults and the seller has the right to cancel the agreement. Sellers are often reluctant to accept a sale of property contingency if the buyer's existing house is not already on the market. Of course, this depends on the house, its location, and the current market.

Contingent sales happen most often when the buyer is relocating from one area to another. The purchase of a new home must be contingent on the sale of the existing house, which can be frustrating for the buyers who may have to end up renting a house until they have an offer on their house.

In this situation, once the buyers have a valid offer and binding purchase and sale agreement on their existing house, they can then make an offer contingent on the closing of their existing house on a new house. There are a number of ways to proceed with the purchase of a new home before the existing house closes: borrow the necessary funds, take out a bridge loan, or receive a "gift" from a family member.

If you have sufficient funds in your 401(k) account, you can borrow funds from it to make a down payment or you may borrow money using a secured loan using any asset (a car, stocks, bonds, insurance policy, or the like) for collateral. You may even qualify for a line of credit against your existing house's equity. A bridge loan is made against the equity the buyers' should get from their existing house when it closes. The proceeds from a bridge loan must be used to make a down payment and pay the closing costs of buying a new house. All of these options are costly in terms of fees and interest and should be used only as a shortterm solution, until the existing house closes.

> *If you have sufficient funds in your 401(k) account, you can borrow funds from it to make a down payment.*

Inspection Contingencies

Although we have mentioned inspection contingencies before, they bear repeating. This type of contingency is the most commonly made. When you make an offer contingent upon inspections, you are saying, in effect, "I want to buy this house, but I really want my experts to go over it first," which seems like a reasonable request. If a seller refuses to accept an offer contingent upon inspection, you should definitely look for another house.

Within the agreed upon time for the inspections, they should be performed. Only the buyer (and their agent) should see the result. If there are any surprises in the report that suddenly make the house less attractive to you, your agent should notify the seller or the seller's agent that you are voiding the contract due to inspection issues.

Buyer's Obligations

If you have made an offer on a house, you can withdraw the offer, without penalty, anytime until the seller accepts the offer. Once the seller accepts the offer, all of the stipulations of the agreement are in force. At this point, you cannot breach the contract without some penalty.

The buyer may be held responsible (in court) for any expenses incurred by the seller as a result of the offer, acceptance, and contract. For example, in some areas, once the contract is in force, the seller owes a commission to the selling agent, regardless of the outcome of the transaction. Because these commissions are typically 6 or 7 percent of the selling price (the accepted offer price), depending on the price of the home, this is likely a substantial amount for the seller to pay without the sale of the house providing income. In this situation, it is likely that in addition to claiming the earnest money, the seller will sue the buyer to recoup the commission and any other costs he or she had because of the breached contract.

Question 14

My Offer Was Accepted: Now What?

When you have made an offer to buy a home and the offer has been accepted, and any contingencies in the offer have expired, the purchase and sale agreement moves toward closing and the delivery of the house to the buyer. The contract may detail certain pieces of property that are not included in the sale, but without this type of a statement, the law is very clear on what is and isn't a part of the sale, in the absence of language to the contrary. After the offer is accepted, inspections must be done and the lender will want an appraisal of the property.

What Can the Seller Remove From the House?

Real estate law is fairly consistent that when a buyer makes an offer to buy a home, the offer includes the real property, meaning the land and everything attached to it, such as houses, garages, barns, fences, and other improvements. However, it also includes everything affixed or attached to the houses, garages, barns, such as curtain rods, window treatments, lighting fixtures, built-in appliances, doors, certain machinery, and so on.

If a seller wishes to remove any items from the home, he or she must detail these items in the purchase and sale agreement, as a form of counteroffer to the buyer (assuming these items were unknown to the buyer at the time of the offer). If the buyer and seller can agree to the exclusion of certain items from the sale, the seller then has the right to remove these items from the property. Otherwise the buyer assumes ownership of all real property.

Inspections

If any part of the purchase and sale agreement is contingent on one or more inspections, these inspections should be ordered after the seller has accepted the buyer's offer. If the purchase and sale agreement is not contingent on inspection, there is no reason to have the house inspected and you are essentially buying the house "as is."

The sole purpose of house inspections is to provide you with better information about the condition of the house. Depending on how detailed or exact you want the information to be, you can hire specialists to separately inspect the structure, wiring, plumbing, and for insect damage (termites, carpenter ants, and the like). However, a general building inspector may be able to cover all of the structure and its infrastructure (except for the pest inspection, which usually requires a specialist). The inspector is working for you, so let him or her know your concerns and the specific areas of the home that should receive more attention.

Some inspections are required by the local city, county, or state laws, such as insect or pest inspections and hazardous gases inspections. Pest infestation inspections are intended to identify structural or health threats from insects or rodents. Hazardous gases inspections test for dangerous gases that could threaten the health and safety of a house's occupants. These gases are primarily radon (a naturally occurring, invisible, colorless, odorless, radioactive gas) and carbon monoxide. This inspection typically looks at a home's furnace, flue, and fireplace to ensure that they are properly ventilated.

Make sure you get a written inspection report from each inspection you have done. If you wish to present any findings to the seller, you will need the official report from the inspector as your backup documentation.

If the inspections find any serious problems (and what that means is strictly up to you) and your purchase offer was made contingent on inspection, you now have the option of exercising your contingency and voiding the contract, asking the seller to repair the items, or setting aside the findings of the inspections and proceeding with the transaction.

If you decide to opt out of the purchase, the contract is voided, your earnest money is returned, the house is back on the market, and you are once again looking for a house to buy. If you ask the seller to repair certain items and he or she refuses to do so, you can forget it and proceed with the purchase or choose to void the contract. If you want the house so badly that you will accept its faults, then the contingency will expire and the purchase proceeds.

Make sure you have a written inspection report from every inspection you have done.

Appraisals

The mortgage lender with whom you are working will want to have an appraisal performed on the house you are buying to ensure that the fair market value of the house is at least the same or more than what you've asked to borrow from the lender. Should you not pay the lender as agreed, the lender will repossess the property and attempt to sell it to recoup its funds. If the house isn't worth the loan amount, the lender will be making a bad loan.

Typically, the lender's appraisal comes later in the process nearer to closing. Unless you are seeking a loan from a governmental program (such as FHA or VA), the appraiser returns only the fair market value of the house and its property. The appraisal will have very little else in the way of information about the property.

Question 15

How Do I Choose a Mortgage Lender?

We wish we could tell you that finding a mortgage lender is the easiest and less stressful part of buying a house, but we can't honestly do so. There are ethical, honest mortgage lenders in the marketplace, but there are also unethical, dishonest, misleading, and disreputable lenders out there that promise sunshine but deliver only rain.

Shopping for a Mortgage Lender

Dr. Jack Guttentag of the University of Pennsylvania has developed a Website called The Mortgage Professor (*www.mtgprofessor.com*) on which you can find a virtual encyclopedia on mortgage brokers and how to choose one. Click on the Table of Contents link to access a list of mortgage and homebuying tutorials, including one to help you decide if you should personally shop for a mortgage lender or use the services of a mortgage broker.

If the outcome of this test is that you should use the services of a mortgage broker, then you should probably use the services of what is called an up-front mortgage broker. An up-front mortgage broker is so called because he or she collects his or her fee "upfront," typically as a fixed fee that won't change during the search.

Conventional Mortgage Brokers

A conventional mortgage broker makes his money through a variety of front-end and back-end fees.

➲ **Front-end fees:** These fees are charged on the loan as one or more fees, including Loan Origination Fee, Application Fee, Processing Fee, Administration Fee, and perhaps even a Mortgage Broker Fee. These fees are revenue for the mortgage broker and should be negotiable on the loan. Front-end fees must be stated in full on the Good Faith Estimate statement the broker is required to give you.

➲ **Back-end fees:** Back-end fees are based on a rate schedule that lists the mortgage rates available from a lender and the premium or cost associated with each rate.

There are actually two different types of back-end fees a mortgage broker can earn from arranging your mortgage loan with a lender:

➡ **Yield-Spread Premium (YSP):** A mortgage broker is paid an amount depending on whether he is able to sell the mortgage loan with an interest rate higher than the wholesale interest rate. For example, if the wholesale (also called "par") rate is 6.00 percent, and the broker is able to sell the loan (lock the borrower in at a certain rate) at 6.125 percent, the mortgage broker will be paid a bonus of about 0.5 percent; at 6.250 percent, the broker earns a 1 percent premium payment. On a $200,000 loan, a 0.5 percent bonus is $1,000 and a 1 percent bonus is $2,000. The higher the interest rate on the loan above the par rate, the more the broker makes.

➡ **Service Release Premium (SRP):** If the loan the borrower is seeking is to be guaranteed by the Federal Housing Administration (FHA), the Veterans Administration (VA), or the United States Department of Agriculture's Rural Loans programs, the broker is able to earn another back-end payment on top of anything earned from an YSP.

Up-front Mortgage Brokers

Unlike a conventional mortgage broker, an *up-front mortgage broker* (UMB) makes his or her money directly from you in the form of a negotiated fee that is established "up-front" before his or her services are provided. Some UMBs charge a percentage of the mortgage amount; some have a fixed-fee schedule based on the loan amount.

The UMB shops the mortgage lender market for you, using the same financial and personal information each lender would ask of you. Because a UMB is constantly in contract with lenders, she is more likely to know about or be able to dig out a special loan program from which you would benefit.

Conventional mortgage brokers may quote lower rates than a UMB, but then charge points to arrange the loan. A UMB will quote you an honest, straightforward rate.

Finding a Mortgage Lender Yourself

If you believe you are able to shop for a mortgage lender yourself, you should go about it in a systematic, objective way. Before you begin looking for a mortgage lender, you should decide the type of mortgage loan program you'll accept, the term of the loan, whether you are willing to pay points to get a lower rate, the amount available for your down payment, and how long of a lock period you need.

Once you have developed your preferences, you can then begin talking with potential mortgage lenders and visiting their Websites.

Any mortgage lender with whom you speak should willingly provide you with the names and telephone numbers of customers whose situations were similar to yours. They should also be willing to state how long they have been in business, how they are compensated, and how a rate lock is handled.

> *The longer you wish to hold an interest rate, the more it will cost in points added to the loan.*

Rate Locks

Before you can go through closing on a mortgage loan, you have to lock in an interest rate. The components of a rate lock are the type of loan program you are using, the interest rate you wish to lock, the points you have agreed to pay, and the length (days) of the lock you are seeking.

As a rule of thumb, the longer you wish to hold (lock in) an interest rate, the more it will cost in points added to the loan. If you are afraid the interest rate may go up before you close, depending on how high you think the rate may go, you will want to lock in the interest rate. The points (or the lender may insist on a slightly higher rate) charged by the lender depends on how the lender expects the rate to change. If the lender expects the rate to go lower, then they will not charge too much to lock in the current rate; however, if the lender expects the rate to increase, they will be looking to make up the revenue lost by allowing you to lock in a lower rate. Unless the rate drops substantially below the locked rate, most lenders aren't willing to release the lock to allow you to close at a lower rate.

For example, if you are looking for 15-day (meaning 15 business days) lock at 6.00 percent on a 30-year fixed rate mortgage, the lender might charge 2 points. At the end of the 15-day period, if closing doesn't occur, the lock expires and the rate lock is cancelled. Most lenders will lock the rate again, but typically at the current interest rates and points schedule. Under these same terms, a 30-day lock might cost 2.25 points and a 60-day lock might cost 2.50 points. Another option is to lock in at a slightly higher interest rate to avoid or minimize the points charged.

Many mortgage brokers and even mortgage lenders pay games with locking in an interest rate, hoping to make more money on the deal. If you verbally instruct a mortgage broker to lock in your rate and the broker verbally confirms the rate is locked, the rate may not be, in fact, locked. The broker may be hoping the rate will drop, at which time, the broker can then lock in the lower rate and profit from the difference. If this plan backfires on the broker, any number of administrative problems, paperwork glitches, or other issues can cause your rate lock to expire before you are able to close.

Get It in Writing

Make absolutely sure that you get everything in writing when it concerns your mortgage, rate lock, and the points and fees on the loan. Every legitimate lender will provide you with a loan commitment letter that includes the lender's name, the interest rate, the date the rate was locked, the date the lock expires, and any and all fees and points that are associated with the loan.

Mortgage Applications

Mortgage applications are among the most difficult application forms most people ever encounter. The information asked for on the application is needed by the lender to fully develop a profile of how willing and able you are to pay back any money it might loan you. Think about it, if you were loaning somebody a hundred thousand dollars, wouldn't you want to know quite a bit about the person to whom you are loaning the money?

There is a considerable amount of paperwork involved with obtaining a mortgage loan. The application form establishes your employment record, your credit information, the amount you are looking to borrow, and the address of the property you wish to buy. Along with this information, the lender will likely ask you for supporting documentation, such as copies of your income tax returns, pay stubs, copies of your monthly bill statements, and the like.

The lender will verify your credit standing with the three major credit bureaus to learn whether you pay your bills on time. A poor credit rating may be enough for a lender to reject your application.

If you are new to mortgage applications, get help filling it in. Work with a loan officer or your mortgage broker to complete the application.

Mortgage Loan Approvals

The stages of a mortgage loan's approval are:

- ➲ **Prequalified:** Prequalified means that you and a lender have determined a house price you can afford to pay based on the amount you have to use for the down payment, the total of your debts, and your income. In effect, prequalification indicates that you would probably qualify for a mortgage loan, without any guarantees. If you work with a lender to get prequalified, be sure to get a prequalification letter.

- ➲ **Preapproval:** Preapprovals happens after you have submitted a mortgage loan application detailing the house you wish to buy, the price of the house, your down payment, your gross monthly income, your total monthly bills, and your credit information. Preapproval is based on your debt-to-income ratio, which should be less than 36 percent, if you are looking for a good interest rate and your FICO (Fair, Isaac, and Co.) credit score. Preapproval establishes the house price and monthly payment you are conservatively qualified to pay. Preapproval is not binding to either the borrower or the lender.

➲ **Final approval:** Once the borrower has met all of the lender's requirements and the conditions for closing, the loan is approved.

Good-Faith Estimate

When you are preapproved for a mortgage loan, your lender should provide you with a good-faith estimate of what fees, costs, and other money you will be responsible to pay at closing. This allows you to verify that the lender has, in fact, made good on all of the promises it made when you were shopping for the loan. It also allows you to gather your funds together so that you have the correct amount for closing.

It is best to get a good-faith estimate from a lender before you make any commitments to the lender. If you determine any anomalies between what you were expecting and what is listed on the good-faith estimate, bring it to the lenders attention immediately for correction.

Q*uestion* **16**

Which Type of Mortgage Is Best for Me?

Unfortunately, there are several different types of mortgage plans available on the market. In fact, several of the different mortgage plans have variations within themselves. So, how do you know which type of mortgage is best for you? It really depends on your finances, your credit, your status, your future plans, and your preferences.

This chapter provides an overview of the mortgage options you are most likely to encounter as you search for a lender and a mortgage loan.

Types of Mortgages

There can be some confusion in the various names and terms used to describe the different types of mortgage programs. Some of the more common mortgage types you will encounter in the marketplace are:

➲ **Conforming loan:** A conforming loan that meets all of the criteria, limits, and qualifications of the largest mortgage loan buyers, the Federal National Mortgage Association (FNHA—"Fannie Mae") and the Federal Home Loan Mortgage Corporation (FHLMC—"Freddie Mac"). These agencies buy and resell mortgages that "conform" to their criteria. The current (2005) loan limit for Fannie Mae and Freddie Mac loans is $359,650.

➲ **Non-conforming loan:** A mortgage loan that doesn't meet the criteria of Fannie Mae or Freddie Mac because of its loan amount, interest rate, or the amount of points associated with it. A non-conforming loan typically has looser requirements than a conforming loan, but also carries a higher interest rate. A type of non-conforming loan that is becoming more common is a jumbo loan, which is a loan for an amount greater than the conforming loan limits. Jumbo loans typically carry a slightly higher interest rate than a conforming loan.

➲ **Conventional loan:** A conventional loan is any mortgage loan that is not guaranteed or backed by a governmental program, agency, or department.

➲ **Governmental loan:** A mortgage loan made under one of the various governmental loan guarantee programs, such as the Federal Housing Administration (FHA), the Veterans Administration (VA), or the Rural Housing Service (RHS).

Mortgage Plans

Each lender typically has several mortgage plan options to offer, depending on your credit and financial capabilities. A mortgage plan differs from a mortgage type in that there are often several mortgage plans offered within one mortgage type. For example, there are any numbers of conforming, conventional loan programs. FHA also has more than one mortgage plan.

Fixed-Rate Mortgages

A fixed-rate mortgage (FRM) is a mortgage loan for which the interest rate remains the same over the term of the loan. FRMs have been the standard mortgage type over the past couple of centuries and are still fairly popular. FRMs do offer some flexibility in the length of the term, with the term ranging from 10 to 30 years commonly. Longer-term FRMs are available, with terms up to as much as 45-months, but these are rare. The most commonly offered FRMs have terms of either 30 or 15 years. The trade-off in an FRM is that shorter-term loans have lower interest rates.

For example, a 15-year FRM for $100,000 with an interest rate of 5 percent would have a monthly principal and interest payment of about $790. Over the term of this loan, you would pay more than $42,000 in total interest. A 30-year FRM for $100,000 with an interest rate of 5.75 (longer term—higher interest) would have a monthly payment of about $585, which is considerably lower than the 15-year FRM's payment amount. Over the life of the 30-year loan, the total interest paid would be over $110,000, more than 2.5 times as much.

Obviously, the choice between shorter and longer term FRMs is a choice of lower monthly payments versus paying less interest and having the loan paid off in a shorter time frame. If you are considering an FRM and you can afford the higher payments, you may want to choose a shorter term.

FHA Loans

The Federal Housing Administration (the FHA) is a part of the U.S. Department of Housing and Urban Development (HUD) and manages a variety of mortgage loan programs. In general, FHA loan programs offer a lower down payment and qualification requirements, but have some requirements on the type and condition of the houses on which an FHA loan can be made.

The focus in all of the FHA mortgage programs is to help low- to middle-income homebuyers in purchasing adequate housing by underwriting mortgage insurance for loans made by commercial mortgage lenders. The typical FHA buyer is a first-time homebuyer or other homebuyers who may not be able to meet the loan requirements of most lenders without some assurance that they are protected.

FHA Mortgage Insurance Programs

To assist both the buyer and the seller, the FHA provides mortgage insurance to the lender to lessen the lender's risk in making a loan to an FHA buyer. Should the borrower default on the loan, FHA's mortgage insurance pays off the loan and the buyer is then in default to FHA. The insurance is purchased from FHA by the borrower at closing. Depending on the loan, one or two types of mortgage insurance (or both in some cases) are required:

➲ **One-time mortgage insurance premium (OTMIP):** If this format is used, 2 percent of the loan amount (for 15-year mortgages) or 2.25 percent of the loan amount (for longer-term loans) is paid at closing or added to the amount borrowed. Many of the FHA mortgage programs also require an annual premium along with the OTMIP.

➲ **Annual mortgage insurance premiums (AMIP):** This type of mortgage insurance requires an annual payment (up front) of 0.5 percent of the unpaid balance each year for the life of the loan. Typically, the annual premium is paid in installments with partial payments made each month.

To qualify for an FHA mortgage loan program, a buyer must have a good credit rating, the money required for closing, and steady and sufficient income to make the monthly payments, and be working with a lender approved by HUD for the FHA programs. However, there are first-time buyer and other types of programs that can limit the down payment amount to 3 percent or include the closing costs in the mortgage loan itself. An FHA loan doesn't include a prepayment penalty. This allows the borrower to pay off the loan early by making larger than normal payments. Prepayment penalties, which charge a small percentage of the unpaid balance for paying off the loan before its term or within a certain time period, are becoming a common feature of many adjustable rate and fixed-rate mortgages.

FHA loans typically have interst rates at or slightly above the market interst rate for mortgages.

FHA Mortgage Loan Limits

FHA programs are available for houses located in both urban and rural settings that are one- to four-family structures, and for the purchase of a condominium (condo). The primary requirement for a qualifying house is that it be the buyer's primary residence. FHA loans typically have interest rates at or slightly above the market interest rate for mortgages, but most FHA buyers are willing to trade a slightly higher interest rate for a lower down payment.

FHA loans are available only for houses that meet the statutory limit set by HUD for a particular state, county, city, or area (in some rare cases). The statutory limit prescribes the upper lending limit (maximum mortgage amount) for various size structures in a particular area.

Loan limits do vary in different parts of the country, depending on the prevailing house prices in an area. When you are looking for a house in your area and want to use an FHA mortgage loan program for the financing, be sure you know the statutory limit in your area (your agent and the lenders should know), because that is the highest loan amount you can borrow.

FHA Qualification Criteria

Two ratios are primary keys to qualifying for an FHA loan program: housing expense to income ratio and debt to income ratio.

Housing Expense to Income Ratio

Most lenders require a maximum ratio of 29 percent between the projected total housing expense, which includes the mortgage payment (principal and interest) and any escrow deposits (for property taxes, hazard insurance, mortgage insurance, etc.), and your gross monthly income. In other words, your projected mortgage payment divided by your gross monthly income should be 29 percent or less.

For example:

Projected total monthly housing expense
(mortage payment): $1,250

Total gross monthly income
(husband and wife): $5,250

$1,250 divided by $5,250 = 23.8 percent

In this case, this couple meets the Housing Expense to Income ratio requirement, which should encourage the lender to move forward and look at their credit score and a few other calculations, such as their debt to income ratio.

Debt to Income Ratio

Where the housing expense to income ratio indicates that the total cost of housing should not exceed 29 percent of total gross income, this ratio determines how much of the borrower's gross income their total amount of debt (including all other monthly payments) represents.

94

To calculate the debt to income ratio, calculate the total of all monthly installment and credit payments (including the estimated monthly housing expense) and divide this total by the total gross income. For example:

Total monthly debt amount: $1,700

Husband and wife gross monthly income: $4,250

1,850 divided by 4,250 = 40.0 percent

The maximum ratio used for the debt to income ratio is 41 percent, meaning that no more than 41 percent of gross monthly income should be required to pay the total monthly debts.

VA Loans

VA loans, as they are commonly called, are similar to FHA loans, except that the loan is guaranteed by the U.S. Department of Veterans Affairs and only service veterans and members of the U.S. armed forces can qualify.

In effect, the VA program guarantees the equivalent of a healthy down payment for the lender. The current program has a maximum guarantee amount equal to 25 percent of the Federal Home Loan Mortgage Corporation (Freddie Mac) conforming loan limit for a single family house, which is $359,650 for the year 2005. Which means the VA maximum guarantee amount is $89,912 and the maximum loan amount for a zero down loan is the same as that for Freddie Mac ($359,650). A VA loan has no monthly mortgage insurance premiums and limits the amount of the closing cost the buyer must pay.

However, not every member or veteran of the armed forces is automatically qualified for a VA guaranteed loan. Borrowers must still satisfy the credit rating and ratios tests that are required of FHA borrowers.

Note: Several states, such as California, Oregon, and Wisconsin, have state-supported programs to help veterans get mortgage loans to purchase single-family housing.

Rural Housing Service (RHS)

Perhaps the largest of the other governmental mortgage loan guarantee program is the RHS program. RHS, a department of the U.S. Department of Agriculture, was created to guarantee loans by commercial lenders for the purchase of rural housing by low- to middle-income buyers.

To qualify for the program a rural resident cannot have a total income that exceeds more than 115 percent of the area median family income (AMFI) for the area. Some areas around the country have higher median incomes than others. Understand that a median income is not an average, but the center-most income when the family incomes of an area are ranked low to high.

The purpose of the RHS program is to rural residents to purchase modestly priced housing as their primary residence, which can be an existing structure or new construction with a 30-year loan with no required down payment amount. The loan proceeds can be used to purchase and repair an existing and newly constructed dwelling.

Median income is ...the center-most income when the family incomes of an area are ranked high to low.

State and Local Housing Programs

Several states, counties, and even cities have governmental or government-private business partnership programs aimed at helping low- to moderate-income families to obtain satisfactory housing. Many of these programs are specifically designed to help first-time homebuyers, displaced workers and homemakers, and single-parent families. These programs are typically more lenient on the qualification guidelines and often designed with lower up-front fees.

Adjustable Rate Mortgages

An adjustable rate mortgage (ARM) is the type of mortgage loan that allows its interest rate to fluctuate throughout the term of the loan, which of course causes the monthly payment amount to fluctuate as well. An ARM loan typically offers a lower payment in the initial periods of the loan, sometimes artificially low, which causes the rate to be called a *teaser rate*. Teaser rates are generally offered for a relatively short period of time, such a one month, three months, or one year. An ARM is most commonly available with 30-year terms, but there are some available at 15 years, as well.

The interest rate in an ARM loan is typically tied to (indexed to) a particular publicly reported index. Which index is used in a particular loan is defined at the time the loan is made. The indices used most commonly to control the interest rate on an ARM loan have names such as CODI, COFI, COSI, CMT, MTA, and RNY. If you are considering an ARM loan, be sure you know what index the loan will be using and that you understand how the index is calculated and its volatility.

The interest rate in an ARM is recalculated at preset time intervals according to the loan's specifics. A commonly used adjustment period is annually, and the rate for the upcoming year would be calculated something like this:

Interest rate = Index rate + Margin rate

The index rate is supplied by the index type used by the ARM program. One commonly used index is a *prime rate index*. A bank's prime rate is the interest rate it charges its very best (and largest) depositors. So, to calculate the new rate on an ARM the prime rate (say, 3.5 percent) is added to the fixed percentage points specified in the ARM loan. For example, this type of ARM is commonly explained as a "prime plus 3.9 percent" loan or something similar. In this case, the new interest rate would be:

$$\text{Interest rate} = \text{Index rate} + \text{Margin rate}$$
or
$$7.4\% = 3.5\% + 3.9\%$$

The index is the fluctuating value in this calculation and the margin remains constant throughout the term of the loan.

One safety valve built into an ARM to protect the borrower is an interest rate cap. The interest rate cap limits the amount of increase the rate can jump in one year as well as over the life of the loan. In each case, meaning the annual rate cap and the loan rate cap, if the index rate is greater than the applicable rate cap, the rate cap is used to calculate the new interest rate. For example, in the previous example, if the rate cap for the life of the loan was 3.0 percent, then the new rate would be 6.9 percent.

However, some ARMs use a payment cap instead of a rate cap, which limits the payment amount and not the interest rate. While this may sound better at first blush, what can happen is that while the payment may not be able to rise above a certain payment level, if the interest rate continues to climb, the payment amount may not be sufficient to cover all of the interest due each month. The end result is that the excess (unpaid) interest is added to the loan, increasing the total to be paid. This type of loan is known as a *negatively amortizing loan.*

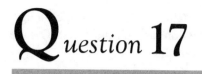

Q*uestion* 17

Are There Programs for First-Time Homebuyers?

You may be surprised to learn that first-time homebuyer doesn't necessarily refer to someone who has never purchased a home before. In fact, in most programs set up to assist first-time buyers, the criteria typically required is only that you haven't owned a home for at least three years (and even only two years in some cases).

So, if you have never owned a home, haven't owned one for two to three years, have become a single parent, or a displaced homemaker recently, you will more than likely qualify for one of the first-time homebuyer programs available in the mortgage loan market.

Governmental Assistance Programs

Most of the programs available to help first-time buyers, like those described in this section, are administered by state agencies and local housing authorities.

> *The MCC can be used with almost every type of mortgage loan, including FRM, ARM, FHA, and VA loans.*

Mortgage Credit Certificate

Many of these programs require the buyer to apply for and receive a Mortgage Credit Certificate (MCC) that certifies the buyer is a first-time home buyer (has not owned a home in the past three years). The MCC also provides certain discounts and federal and state tax breaks. Each state or city housing authority that issues MCCs uses a local formula to compute the amount of credit for which the borrower qualifies.

The MCC credit reduces the borrower's federal income tax liability as a function the amount of mortgage interest they pay during the tax year. Borrowers receive an income tax credit of either 15 or 20 percent (depending on their income and the property purchased) of the mortgage interest paid during the tax year. The additional income helps the buyer to increase their net income during the year and can help them afford a bit more house. The MCC can be used with almost every type of mortgage loan, including conventional, fixed-rate mortgages (FRM), adjustable-rate mortgages (ARM), FHA, and VA loans. However, there are some loan programs with which an MCC cannot be used. Be sure to ask your lender or real estate agent whether the use of an MCC is permitted on the mortgage programs you are considering.

State-Level Programs

Every state in the United States has an agency that is responsible for assisting low- to moderate-income and first-time homebuyers with a variety of programs that provide down payment assistance, closing cost discounts, and lower interest rate mortgage programs. These agencies focus on providing assistance and promoting home ownership for first-time homebuyers, anyone looking to buy a home in an urban area, and people wanting to buy a house who don't have money for a down payment.

The programs offered by the housing finance agencies typically have strict income and home price ceilings and target their programs to assisting those who truly need assistance rather than the general public. If you are looking to buy a house and you think you need and may qualify for a little bit of help in obtaining financing, the place to start is at your state (or city) housing finance agency or authority, before you talk with a lender or a real estate agent.

City, Association, Union, and Tribal Assistance Programs

Many cities, trade associations, labor unions, and Native American tribal associations also have a variety of housing assistance programs for first-time buyers and in many cases rebuyers as well. You should contact these agencies, associations, and groups directly for information. Lenders and your real estate agent should also be able to help you to obtain information about these programs.

First-Time Buyer Mortgage Programs

There are literally dozens of different first-time buyer programs available in the marketplace. Some are dedicated to helping only true first-timers and others will assist others who haven't owned a home for a few years. In fact, we'd venture to say that there is just about a first-time buyer assistance program for a buyer in just about every possible financial need situation.

The first-time buyer has a range of mortgage options available that include zero-down payment programs and 3- and 5-percent-down payment programs for a variety of mortgage plans.

Zero-Down Programs

There is only limited numbers of basic zero-down loan programs available to first-time homebuyers. The most common of these programs are:

No Down Payment FRM

This mortgage loan program requires no down payment, but the borrower must have excellent credit (660 or higher), and have the funds to pay closing costs. This type of loan is also available as a 5/1 (fixed for five years and then adjusted each one year) or a 7/1 (fixed for seven years and then adjusted each one year) ARM as well. The Fannie Mae Flex 100-percent loans are examples of this type of zero-down loan.

Combination Loans

A combination loan, also called a piggyback or an 80/20 loan, combines a first mortgage with a second mortgage. In this type of loan, a first mortgage covers 80 percent of the purchase price of a home and a second mortgage is written to provide the funds for a 20 percent down payment, eliminating PMI (private mortgage insurance) on the loan. The first and second mortgages are paid separately, sometimes to the same lender and sometimes to different lenders. To qualify for this loan, the borrower must have a credit score of 660 or higher.

Shared Appreciation Mortgage (SAM) Loans

In this type of a loan, any loaned amounts are like a second mortgage. However, a SAM is a zero-interest loan that is deferred with no required payments until the house is sold or the first mortgage is paid off. At that time, a percentage of any appreciation in the home's value, based on a formula, is paid to the lender. For example, if a buyer needs to borrow an amount equal to 17 percent of the purchase price of a home, when the house is sold, the lender is paid the original loan amount plus 17 percent of any excess funds above the original purchase price, after expenses.

100 Percent Plus Loans

In addition to being zero-down mortgages, these programs allow the borrower to add closing costs and even other debts to the mortgage. The most typical of these programs are the *103 percent* programs intended for first-time home buyers. However, a very good credit score (600 or higher) is required to qualify.

> *With interest-only loans, you will pay only the interst due on the unpaid pricipal balance.*

Interest-Only Loans

Actually, there is no such thing as an interest-only mortgage loan. However, most types of mortgages offer an interest-only option and whether this is right for you depends on, well, you. If you would like to pay a slightly lower payment amount during the first few years of the mortgage, you may want to choose an interest-only option, if one is available. What this means is that instead of paying a fully amortizing payment, you will pay only the interest due on the unpaid principal balance. Because you are paying only interest, the principal amount never changes, so the amount of interest you pay each month remains the same during the interest-only period of the loan. When you decide to begin paying towards the principal, you will be, in effect, amortizing the loan over its remaining term, which will always result in a higher payment.

Occupation-Based Loans

Some states and cities offer special mortgage programs or assistance to certain occupations in an effort to entice them to live in the community in which they work. The more common of these programs are available for teachers and police officers, but there are also similar programs for firefighters and other emergency services personnel. The assistance offered varies, but is typically a lower interest rate mortgages with down payment and closing cost assistance packages either as loans or grants.

The Veterans Affairs (VA) mortgage loan program is available to qualified veterans of the U.S. armed forces, the reserves, and the National Guard. The VA program guarantees the equivalent of a down payment as well as other buyer assistance features.

Low-Down-Payment Programs

There are a variety of 3- to 5-percent loans available geared especially toward the first-time homebuyer. In these programs, the source of the funds to be used as a down payment is more flexible than in a conventional loan. In fact, the entire down payment can be gift money or borrowed from a down payment assistance program, which are not options for most conventional programs. These loans are available through most lenders under programs sponsored by the FHA and other guarantors.

Question 18

Why Is My Mortgage Payment So High?

Many homebuyers, especially first-time homebuyers, are surprised that their monthly house payments are as high as they are. Their surprise is because they have forgotten or don't understand all of the components that are present in the monthly mortgage payment.

Components of the Mortgage Payment

The four primary components of a mortgage payment, which are collectively referred to as PITI, are: principal, interest, taxes, and insurance.

Mortgage Principal

Principal is the money you have borrowed and are repaying. Each month a certain portion of your payment is applied to the remaining balance of the amount owed. The amount of your payment that is applied to the principal is not the same amount throughout the life of the loan. In the beginning, the principal payment is actually fairly small and increases as the interest paid is based on a smaller principal balance. The following amortization (the gradual retirement of a debt) table illustrates how the principal portion of a mortgage payment increases over time.

In a 15-year mortgage loan for $275,000 at 6 percent, the principal and interest amounts for various payments during the lifetime of the loan are as follows:

Payment Number	Principal	Interest	Balance
1	945.61	1,375.00	274,054.39
12	998.93	1321.67	263,335.41
24	1,060.55	1,260.06	250,951.38
36	1,125.96	1,194.65	237,803.53
48	1,195.41	1,125.20	223,844.75
96	1,518.75	801.86	158,852.56
132	1,817.46	503.15	98,812.15
180	2,309.06	0.00	0.00

Notice how in the above table, the portion of the $2,320.61 payment applied to the principal balance increases with each payment made and the portion applied to the interest decreases. To understand why this is, we need to talk about how the interest amount is calculated.

Mortgage Interest

The calculations shown in the previous table for the interest portion of each mortgage payment are based on the borrower making exactly the same *principal and interest* (P&I) payment every month. If the borrower were to alter the payment amount or schedule, the amounts for the remainder of the loan would need to be adjusted, even if only slightly. Mortgage interest is calculated either monthly (12 times a year) or daily (365 times a year).

Property Taxes

Property taxes are paid either once or twice a year in nearly all taxing authorities. Many lenders wish to have borrowers pay their property taxes to an escrow (trust) account from which the taxes are paid when they are due. In general, one-twelfth of the annual property tax bill is collected each month and held in the escrow account. When the taxes are due, the lender pays the tax authority for you from the escrow account.

Hazard Insurance

If you are unable to put down at least 20 percent of the purchase price of a home, there will be a mortgage insurance requirement on the loan. The reason for *private mortgage insurance* (PMI) is to cover the amount of the loan normally guaranteed by FHA, VA, or another mortgage loan guarantor.

However, during the life of the loan, once the value of the home exceeds 80 percent of the remaining loan balance, the PMI requirement expires. For example, after three years of mortgage payments, although there is still 95 percent of the original loan amount remaining, the mortgage balance may be now be less than 80 percent of the market value, eliminating the need for PMI.

> *If you are unable to put down at least 20 percent of the purchase price of the home, there will be a mortgage insurance requirement on the loan.*

Escrow Accounts

Depending on the lender and the size of your down payment, you may or may not be required to pay into an escrow account to cover your insurance and property tax liabilities. If you are, the escrow or reserve payment is bundled into your mortgage payment as the "TI" part of PITI (principle, interest, taxes, insurance).

107

Escrow accounts have advantages and disadvantages. The biggest advantage is that the lender assumes the responsibility of paying your property taxes and your insurance premiums. In most states, the disadvantage is that the lender also has your money for as much as one year and can keep any interest earned on it. However, some states now require the lender to pay interest on the average monthly balance of the escrow account. The amount of your payment into an escrow account is just a bit more complicated than dividing your annual tax and insurance amounts by 12.

ARM Payments

The major advantage of an Adjustable Rate Mortgage (ARM) is its lower payment at the beginning that hopefully grows slowly in amount over the life of the loan. The payments for the standard ARM are adjusted periodically to reflect an increase in the interest rate and perhaps changes in the escrow payment amounts.

One type of ARM, called an *Option ARM*, also provides the flexibility of choosing the type and amount of payment you wish to make in any given month. An option ARM normally offers four types of payments you can make:

➲ **Minimum payment option:** This would be the equivalent of the monthly payment on a fixed-rate mortgage; it is the monthly payment set at the beginning of the mortgage and recalculated each year. The increase in the payment from year to year is controlled by the payment cap.

➲ **Interest-only payment option:** Using the interest-only payment option, you can avoid deferred interest on the loan by paying the interest due that month. Deferred interest is created when the amount of the minimum payment option is not sufficient to cover the interest due. If the interest-only payment would be lower than the minimum payment amount, the interest-only payment is not available.

➲ **30-year amortizing payment option:** This payment option pays both principal and interest based on the calculation using the prior month's interest rate, the current loan balance, and the number of payments remaining on the loan term.

➲ **15-year amortizing payment option:** The 15-year amortizing option repays the loan in half the time and saves half the total interest costs of the 30-year option.

Question 19

What Happens at Closing?

The last step in the process of buying a home is closing; a term we assume comes from the business world phrase, "closing the deal." In some states, closing occurs when all the legal documents are recorded at the county clerk or recorder office. In other states, closing occurs when all of the purchase and sale documents are signed and certified and the monies are paid accordingly.

Despite the fact that closing is when the commissioned or transaction-fee agents and agencies are paid, which is why these folks often want the closing to occur as soon as possible, there is no reason to rush into the closing. You are the one buying the house; if you are unsure of anything, assert yourself until everything is to *your* satisfaction. Remember that you have to live, and for some time, with any mistakes or misunderstandings in the closing documents.

Final Walk-Through

At least 24 hours before your closing appointment, you should perform a final walk-through inspection of the house you are buying. The purpose of this walk-through is to allow you to verify that the seller has moved out and has left the house in the condition specified in writing in the signed purchase and sale agreement or any addendums to the agreement.

During the walk-through is not the time to play Mr. or Ms. Nice Person and let anything fairly major slide by, nor is it the time to go ballistic over tiny flaws that you may not have noticed before. The walk-through should be conducted objectively. If there are major problems, such as damage to the interior or exterior structure or landscaping, missing appliances, fixtures, draperies, carpeting, or the like, or furniture, personal effects, or trash needing to be removed, you can delay the closing until the problem is resolved to your satisfaction or the seller has deposited enough money in an escrow account to pay for repairs, replacement of the missing items, or the removal of contents left behind. This isn't an either-or situation left up to the seller; the choice is yours! If you find yourself in this situation, let your real estate agent fight the battle for you; it is definitely one of the services he or she should provide.

> *If there are major problems, you can delay the closing until the problem is resolved to your satisaction.*

What to Look for in the Final Walk-Through

Your final walk-through is your last chance to avoid any surprises that may pop up after you have completed the purchase of the home. Major problems may actually delay the closing, but you shouldn't overlook a significant problem because of this. In effect, the cost to remedy any problem you overlook is added, in the long run, to the cost of the home.

Make a Checklist

Before making your walk-through, you should develop a checklist of the items that the seller has agreed to repair, replace, or furnish. The checklist should also list the appliances, fixtures, and items the seller has agreed to leave in the home as a part of the sale. If you had the foresight to photograph the home when you first agreed to buy it, concentrating on the carpets, draperies, appliances, and the general condition of the home inside and out, you can compare the photos to the house as it now exists.

The final walk-through isn't an inspection and it isn't the time to get picky. Be reasonable and fair, but do stick up for yourself.

What if the Seller Hasn't Moved Out by Closing?

The final walk-through should be done after the seller has vacated the home; that is, if at all possible. In situations where it was negotiated in the purchase and sale agreement that the seller would remain in the house a few days past closing, or the state or local laws don't require the seller to vacate until after the documents are recorded or all of the funds are transferred, you may have to adjust the walk-through a bit.

If your walk-through must be done with the seller's contents in the home, feel free to move any furniture to complete the walk-through. If you need to check repairs and are unable to do so, or you may be worried about the condition of the home after the seller vacates, you should ask that an amount sufficient to correct your worst fears be put into escrow by the seller. These escrow funds will remain on deposit until you are able to perform your final walk-through of the vacant house or the funds are needed to pay for repairs or replacements to the home identified during your walk-through.

The Closing Process

The closing process should actually begin the day before your closing appointment. You should meet with your real estate agent and ensure that between you, you have all of the documents you should have received since you first made your offer on the home. In nearly every case, these documents should include:

➲ Purchase and sale agreement (earnest money agreement) and addendums, if any.

➲ A copy of the earnest money check.

➲ Copies of the inspection reports.

➲ A copy of the appraisal report.

➲ The good faith estimate from the lender.

➲ Proof of title search and title insurance (if required).

➲ Flood certification (where required).

➲ Proof of homeowner's or hazard insurance.

➲ Proof of private mortgage insurance (if required).

➲ Miscellaneous certificates, such as an MCC, or any other mortgage-related documents.

Should there be any questions during the closing process, having these documents with you allows you to refer back to the original information sources.

Closing Costs

The money you are required to bring to closing covers a variety of fees paid to the lender, the closing agent, all of the third-party service providers (appraisers, inspectors, and so on), the local government, and perhaps a few others as well.

In general, most closing costs can be grouped into three categories: lender fees, third-party fees, and governmental fees.

Lender Fees

Many buyers are unaware that all lender fees are negotiable. The lender isn't likely to admit to this, but they are. In fact, while you are shopping for a mortgage, you should consider and compare the total of each lender's fees along with the interest rate, term, and program.

Lender's fees are not typically bundled into the mortgage and must be paid in cash at closing. The primary lender fees you will likely encounter are:

➲ **Administrative fee:** This fee covers the cost of processing the loan paperwork. In many cases, the processing (checking credit, verifying employment, and so on) is done by a third-party and this fee covers his or her charges.

➲ **Application fee:** This fee covers the lender's cost of processing your application.

➲ **Commitment fee:** It is not unusual for a lender to charge a fee to lock in an interest rate and the terms of the mortgage loan. If you locked in your interest rate, the points, or the terms of the loan, the commitment fee is the charge for doing so.

➲ **Document preparation:** The law permits the lender to charge a fee to cover the cost of preparing or examining certain requirement documents when processing an application for a real estate loan. Typically included in the document preparation fee are:

➡ Fees for title examination, title abstracts, title insurance, any property surveying, and the like.

➡ Fees for preparing all of the documents related to the loan, including deeds, mortgages, and closing or settlement documents.

➡ Any notary or credit reporting fees.

➡ Fees for appraisals, as well as building, pest, or flood hazard inspections.

➥   Any required escrow amounts that are not a finance charge.

➲ **Funding fee:** Only if you are buying your new home using a Veterans Affairs (VA) loan guarantee would you be charged a funding fee. This fee is essentially 2.2 percent of the sale price but as the amount of the down payment increases, the funding fee declines to a minimum of 1.25 percent. However, in a VA loan many other closing fees are not charged. The funding fee takes the place of a loan origination fee and the administrative fee.

➲ **Loan origination fee:** Also commonly called the mortgage broker fee, this fee is the income amount the broker receives for brokering the loan between the buyer and the seller (commonly along with portions of other fees as well).

➲ **Processing fee:** This fee is often collected up front with the application. It is, in effect, the same as the administrative fee or the application fee. Check the closing documents closely to ensure you aren't being charged the fee again.

➲ **Tax service fee:** Typically, the tax service fee is a fixed fee, sometimes discounted for repeat business by some title companies or lenders, charged for verifying that no tax liens exist on the property being purchased.

➲ **Underwriting Fee:** This fee covers the cost of underwriting the loan by the lender and is also called the *administrative fee*, so both should not be charged. This fee, if charged by the lender, cannot be avoided in the majority of cases. However, if the broker is charging an administrative fee or an underwriting fee on top of one by the lender, challenge it; the broker does not participate in these parts of the loan processing.

➲ **Wire transfer fee:** This fee may be charged by the closing agent or the lender to cover the cost of the wire transfers of the funds to the applicable parties and their banks.

Third-Party Fees

The fees in this category have been paid or are due to third-party service providers, such as appraisers, inspectors, attorneys, and the like. The fees you may encounter in your closing are:

➲ **Appraisal Fee:** This is the fee due to a professional appraiser for their review of the house and determining its fair market value. The appraisal is ordered by the lender, but it is a fee you must pay, typically. If you paid an appraisal fee up front to the lender, you absolutely should not pay one during closing.

➲ **Attorney, settlement, or closing fees:** This is the charge from the closing agent for their services in conducting the closing meeting and processing the final paperwork.

➲ **Credit report fee:** Generally, this fee is paid up front when the application is submitted. If no fee was collected at that time, the cost of running your credit reports will be in your closing costs.

➲ **Flood certification fee:** If requested by the lender, an inspection may be done to a house known or suspected to be located in a flood plain, which is an area likely to flood. Although the U.S. government actually determines which areas are flood plains, lenders wish to have this situation verified to determine whether or not flood insurance may be required.

➲ **Inspections and surveys:** These are the fees charged by pest, building, and any other inspectors or a surveyor whose services were ordered by the lender.

➲ **Postage and courier fees:** This is the cost of mailing any documents, sending them by courier, or shipping them with a common carrier, such as UPS or FedEx.

➲ **Title insurance and search fees:** Title insurance protects the lender (and sometimes the borrower) from loss due to a dispute over the title of the property you are purchasing. Title search and examination fees cover the cost of researching the public record for any other title claims to the property.

Governmental Fees

The primary fees collected at closing and paid to government agencies are the fees charged by the local records authority for recording the deed and the mortgage and for all of the local and state taxes that apply to the sale of the home.

Who Participates in Closing?

The process prescribed for closing is defined by law and as such varies from state to state, county to county, and even city to city, in some cases. However, in general, the following individuals or representatives should be present during the closing, at some point:

➲ The buyer (you).

➲ The buyer's real estate agent.

➲ The seller.

➲ The seller's real estate agent.

➲ The closing agent (who works for a title company or a lender in most cases) or an attorney, who specializes in real estate law and/or performs closings.

➲ A title company representative, if he or she isn't the closing agent.

⇝   A representative of the mortgage company, if
he or she isn't the closing agent.

In many states, the title company representative and the mortgage company representative don't actually attend the closing.
They typically will transfer their documents and instructions to
the closing agent in advance. It is also very common that the
buyer and seller will not be present at the same time to sign the
papers and pay their money. It is completely possible to go through
the entire process of buying a house and never meet the sellers.

Once all of the documents are signed and certified and all
funds collected, the closing agent then ensures that the documents are recorded with the local property recording authority
and that all funds are properly distributed.

If you and the seller do attend the same closing meeting,
you may receive copies of the documents at the end of the
meeting. However, in most situations, you will receive copies
of only those documents that don't need to be recorded before
copies are distributed. Most commonly, the documents you will
receive from closing are:

⇝   **HUD-1 Settlement Statement:** This form provides
the detail of all of the costs involved in the sale of a
home. You and the seller both sign this form to ac-
knowledge your agreement of who is responsible for
paying each of the costs along with the amount of
the cost. Before you sign the HUD-1 form, you should
compare it against the good faith estimate you received from the lender. By federal law, you have the
right to review this document for 24 hours before
closing. If you discover what you believe to be a
mistake, take you time in reviewing the document
and call the discrepancy to the attention of the closing agent.

⇝   **Certificate of Occupancy (CO):** This only applies
in new construction. However, if the builder has not

provided this document, you will not be able to move into your new home until one is granted. Be sure you verify that a CO has been issued before you enter into closing.

⊃ **Truth In Lending Act (TILA) Statement:** You should have received a copy of this document as an estimate of the costs, interest rates, and fees associated with your mortgage right after you submitted your application. The final version of this document details all of the fees, points, costs, payments, interest rates, and term of your mortgage loan. Review this and make sure everything is exactly what you expected.

⊃ **Mortgage Note:** This document is the contract between you and the lender to which you are promising to repay the amount of the mortgage loan, according to the agreed upon terms. It should also specify the rights of the borrower and the lender in the event the contract is breached.

⊃ **Deed of Trust:** Also called the mortgage, this document provides the security for the mortgage note by granting a claim against the home to the lender just in case you fail to abide by the terms of the note.

Read all of these documents carefully. We know that the print is small and the language is often confusing, but be sure you understand everything before you sign. If you aren't sure of the meaning of any part of a document, ask. Don't worry about appearing stupid; a brief moment of lost pride may save you hundreds, if not thousands, of dollars in the long run.

Once you have signed all of the papers and have paid all of the money due, closing is completed for you. Depending on your local laws or the agreement you have with the seller, you could take possession that day or, worst case, in a few days. In any regard, you now own a home!

Timing the Closing

Scheduling a closing at just the right time can also save you money, not to mention the tax implications of when a closing is done. The conventional wisdom is that you should schedule your closing for the last day of a month. The reasoning behind this is that the amount of the prepaid interest (of the current month) will be lower because there are fewer days between the closing date and the date of the first payment due.

The downside to this is that the first payment will be due a bit sooner. For example, if you close on March 31st, your first mortgage payment will be due around May 1st, but if you close on April 2nd, the first payment will be due around June 1st. Also consider that the April 2nd closing will require you to pay 30 days of prepaid interest (about one month's payment), which is collected in arrears for the previous month (April). The June payment will include the interest for May.

So, closing at the end of a month may reduce the amount of cash required for closing, but there is no benefit in terms of your immediate cash flow.

There may be some tax benefits to scheduling a late December closing rather than an early January closing. By closing in December, you may be able to take some income tax deductions in that tax year, such as point and prepaid interest. Otherwise, you will have to wait a full year to take these deductions. Your agent or lender should be able to advise you on this. You may want to check with a tax accountant as well before you make any assumptions. The IRS also has information available to help first-time homebuyers on its Website (*www.irs.gov*).

Q*uestion* 20

Yippee! I'm a Homeowner: Now What?

Once you are past the trials and tribulations of closing, you are in a world of good news and bad news. The good news is that you are a homeowner; the bad news is that you are a homeowner. You are now responsible for all of its parts, systems, rooms, roofs, windows, and so on. But, what's to worry, you performed your due diligence and you are well assured you have purchased a wonderful home.

As a homeowner, the primary tasks involved with homeownership are maintaining its property value, keeping it a comfortable place to live, and making sure you live up to the requirements of the mortgage contract.

Every new homeowner's worst nightmare is that after living in the new home for only a few days, a major system, such as the heating or air conditioning, fails. You call a service technician who tells you that it will cost thousands of dollars to replace the system because it cannot be repaired.

You immediately contact your real estate agent because you can't believe you overlooked the seller's disclosure that this system was faulty. However, on the disclosure form, the seller had entered "Don't Know," meaning they have no specific knowledge to its age or problems. You next look at the building inspector's report that says the system is working fine and adequate for the size of the home.

To determine whether or not you have any recourse against the seller, you should contact a real estate attorney. But your best bet is to make a claim against the home warranty the seller purchased for you to sweeten the deal. And if the seller didn't buy a home warranty—why didn't you?

Home Warranties

Many people confuse home warranties with hazard insurance, such as their homeowners' policy, but these two programs are completely different. Homeowner's insurance is primarily hazard insurance purchased to repair or replace the home in the event of a major casualty or catastrophe befalls the house, such as a fire, a hurricane or tornado, an earthquake, a tree, or a truck (or any other rather large object) falling on or running into it.

> *If the seller didn't buy a home warranty—why didn't you?*

A home warranty covers repairs and replacement costs for appliances and other systems in the home. You can also purchase a home warranty program that protects you against the cost of replacement or repairs for the major parts of a home, such as walls, roofs, ceilings, and steps against cracking, falling, or any other unusual action. You can find information about whether you should consider buying a home warranty at eHow.com (*www.ehow.com/ how_5584_determine-you-need.html*). If you decide you need to purchase a home warranty, contact your homeowner's insurance agent who can either sell you a warranty or refer you to a reputable provider.

Home warranties are commonly provided with new construction by the builder, developer, or the selling real estate broker to provide you with the assurance that, should you find anything wrong with the home, due to workmanship or materials, it will be corrected at no expense to you. However, home warranty packages are available for homes of any age. If you insist on a home warranty package on a house as a condition of the sale, either you or the seller (or in shares) must pay for it and the funds are collected at closing.

On average, a standard home warranty package costs between $350 and $450 per year. Adding additional systems, especially systems that are expensive to replace, can run the price up fairly quickly. So, before you add a system to a warranty package, consider its age, condition, and cost to replace before paying the additional funds to cover it.

Covenants, Conditions, and Restrictions

Mainly because we didn't know where else to put this discussion, we've made it the last part of the last chapter. But don't take that to mean that this isn't important stuff. Unless you buy a home that is an old family farm surrounded by a few acres of farm land in a generally rural community, it is likely that the development in which you buy will have a set of covenants, conditions, and restrictions (CC&Rs) in force.

CC&Rs are the governing rules, conditions, guidelines, and limitations that all homeowners (and their tenants and guests) must abide by inside the development. CC&Rs, which are also

123

called bylaws, house rules, and the master deed, are generally drawn up by the developer of a housing tract and then maintained and enforced by a homeowners' association. Because the CC&Rs are a recorded legal document, their contents are legally enforceable by the homeowners' association in court, provided they don't conflict with any applicable laws from a local, county, state, or federal authority.

CC&Rs typically cover such things as lot setbacks, easements, and the aesthetics or curb appeal of the houses in the development, including paint colors, fencing, exterior materials, and the like. They can also address pets, parking, parks, association fees, and whether a property can be rented or not. The rules can be changed by a majority vote of the homeowners, which is generally a problem because of attendance.

If you violate the CC&Rs, the penalties may include a fine, forced compliance, a lawsuit for damages, not to mention the potential problem of fighting with your neighbors. However, if you bear in mind that beneath it all, the members of the homeowners' association are all only trying to protect the value of their homes, which is very likely something you share with them, then you should all be one great big happy family!

Additional Information

Websites

If you need more information, the following Websites are very good sources:

- ➲ U.S. Department of Housing and Urban Development *www.hud.gov/buying/*
- ➲ Educated Home Buyer.com
- ➲ Educated homebuyer.com
- ➲ Fannie Mae Foundation *www.homebuyingguide.com*
- ➲ Freddy Mac *www.freddiemac.com/corporate/buyown/ english/preparing/right_for_you/*
- ➲ Bankrate.com *www.bankrate.com/brm/news/real-estate/ BuyerGuide2004/buyers-guide-home.asp*

- ➲ HomeMortgageGuide.com
  www.homemortgageguide.com
- ➲ TheHomeBuyersGuide.org
  www.thehomebuyersguide.org
- ➲ HSBC Mortgage Corporation
  www.us.hsbc.com/personal/mortgage/
  homebuyersguide/
- ➲ Hapless Home Buyer's Guide (Humor)
  www.madkane.com/haplesshome.html

Books

Here's a list of books that could prove helpful. You should be able to find these books online or at your local bookstore.

Cozzi, Guy. *Real Estate Home Inspection Checklist from A to Z.* Greenwich, Conn.: Nenmar Real Estate Training, 2004.

Eldred, Gary W. *The 106 Mortgage Secrets All Homebuyers Must Learn—But Lenders Don't Tell.* New York: John Wiley and Sons, 2003.

Glink, Ilyce R. *10 Steps to Home Ownership : A Workbook for First-Time Buyers.* New York: Three Rivers Press, 1996.

Guttentag, Jack. *Mortgage Encyclopedia: An Authoritative Guide to Mortgage Programs, Practices, Prices and Pitfalls.* Columbus, Ohio: McGraw Hill, 2004.

Irwin, Robert. *How to Buy a Home When You Can't Afford It.* Columbus, Ohio: McGraw Hill, 2002.

O'Hara, Shelley, and Nancy D. Lewis. *The Complete Idiot's Guide to Buying and Selling a Home.* Upper Saddle River, N.J.: Pearson Education, 2003.

Ordway, Nicholas. *The Absolute Beginner's Guide to Buying a House.* New York, Prima Lifestyles, 2002.

Reed, David. *Mortgages 101: Quick Answers to Over 250 Critical Questions About Your Home Loan.* New York: AMACOM, 2004.

Tyson, Eric, and Ray Brown. *Home Buying for Dummies, 2nd Edition.* Indianapolis, Ind.: John Wiley and Sons, 2001.